How-to
Wire Your Hot Rod

Dennis Overholser

Published by:
Wolfgang Publications Inc.
217 Second Street North
Stillwater, MN 55082
www.wolfpub.com

Legals

First published in 2006 by Wolfgang Publications Inc.,
217 Second Street North, Stillwater MN 55082

The information in this book is true and complete to the best of our
knowledge. All recommendations are made without any guarantee
on the part of the author or publisher, who also disclaim any liabili-
ty incurred in connection with the use of this data or specific details.

We recognize that some words, model names and designations, for
example, mentioned herein are the property of the trademark holder.
We use them for identification purposes only. This is not an official
publication.

ISBN number: 1-929133-30-8

Printed and bound in China

Wire Your Hot Rod

Acknowledgements

Writing a book is quite a challenge. Coming up with words and pictures sounds easy but sometimes can be more difficult than first imagined. Many people have helped along the way by giving advice, time and their patience. When photographing stories, the time to finish a job is extended many times due to the stopping for getting the set right and the taking of pictures.

Painless Performance has helped by furnishing photos and many finished goods parts for new photos. Without a source for electrical components, the task would be much greater.

Several of the employees of Painless have also helped. Kathy Shellenberger helped with the coordination of the text and photos to make it all readable. Brian Montgomery and Jeff Abbott down loaded photos for processing. Dale Armstrong, Joe Armstrong and Lance Packard helped in the wiring stories.

Bob Boudreaux, John Roberts, John Nykaza and James Fox as well as my son Lance, all helped with the text and the installation stories.

Randy Rundle at Fifth Avenue Antique Auto Parts was a great help in the information on 6 volt conversions. His book is a must have for those wanting to do the conversion.

All the folks at Powermaster and Tuff Stuff were a great help with the starter and alternator information and photos.

Autometer, Classic Instruments and Dakota Digital furnished needed photos and information on gauges.

Vintage Air, as well as Flex-A-Lite, furnished needed photos and text on electric fans and air conditioning.

Introduction

Real world answers to real world questions is what this book is all about. Starting with a few basics of DC electrical circuits and progressing through a complete harness install. The photos taken for the book are not studio shots but are simple photos to help tell the story they are illustrating. I have tried to write the text in layman's terms so all can understand. Automotive electrical is voodoo to most people, so the simpler the reading is the better chance one has of understanding what it all means.

I've tried to address the needs of the different segments of our hobby. Street Rods, Classics, Trucks, 4X4's and competition vehicles all have a place in the Hot Rod industry. The style of circuits may differ from a simple roadster compared to the all out custom truck or even the traditional race car, but they still require the same care and patience to insure the job is done correctly.

Electronic Fuel Injection is a part of our everyday lives. Most of us don't give it a second thought when we start our daily driver and take off on another excursion. Adding Fuel Injection to our pride and joy may be another story. It has been 20 years since the last carburetor was installed on the automotive production line. Hopefully the information in this book will help to calm those jittery nerves when you do decide to add the drivability and economy of electronic fuel injection.

The chapter on trouble shooting contains the answers to the most common questions. The list of items that can cause problems in an automobile electrical system is endless. A lot of these solutions came from one-on-one repair sessions and seminars at shows and events. Some were real brain teasers, and some were solved by stepping back and looking at the problem from a different angle.

Regardless of your back ground or level of expertise, I hope this book will be an asset to your library.

Chapter One

Basics of DC Electricity

What is Electricity?

It is not our intention to offer an engineering level text book explanation of DC electronic theory. Rather, this book is intended to serve the individual wiring, or rewiring, a car or truck. With this end goal, we offer here an overview of electronic theory.

WHAT IS ELECTRICITY?

Whether it is a streak of lightning from the sky, 110 volts from a wall socket in the house, or the high energy spark that ignites the fuel in your automotive engine, it's simply voodoo to most people.

You don't need a degree in electrical engineering to wire your hot rod. You do need to use good components, installed with patience and attention to detail.

There are a lot of theories on how and in which direction electricity flows through wires. Some state that electrons flow through the wire and some state they flow around the wire. Of course there's the question of which way the electricity really flows, from positive to negative or negative to positive?

To most people the answer is "who cares as long as my car starts and runs".

To better understand some basics of automotive electrical systems and why they are designed the way they are, there are a few basic terms we must first understand and a theory that most people can understand.

First, the terms:

Voltage: The force that pushes electrons through a wire (sometimes called the electromotive force).

Current: The volume of electrons moving through the wire, measured in amps.

Resistance: The restriction to the flow of electrons, measured in ohms.

Most people have heard of the, "water through the hose theory," where the water pressure is the voltage, the volume of water is the current and the kink in the hose is the resistance.

We offer another theory, the "park bench" theory.

Imagine a park bench, which will represent a wire, just long enough to seat 6 people and each person represents an electron. If someone at one end (the voltage) decides to sit down and is large enough to force the 6 people to shift down the bench, a person at the far end will be forced off the bench. This is electron flow.

Current is the number of people (electrons) being moved during a given period of time. Current is measured in amperage (amps) and is controlled by pressure pushing the people on the bench (voltage), and the resistance to their movement.

Resistance is the force trying to prevent the people

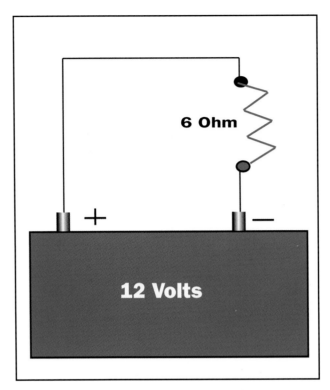

Using Ohm's law (I=V/R) we determine that the current in this impractical circuit is 2 amps.

Length Current	0-4ft.	4-7ft.	7-10ft.	10-13ft.	13-16ft.	16-19ft.
0-20A	14ga.	12ga.	12ga.	10ga.	10ga.	8ga.
20-35A	12ga.	10ga.	8ga.	8ga.	6ga.	6ga.
35-50A	10ga.	8ga.	8ga.	6ga.	6ga.	4ga.
50-65A	8ga.	8ga.	6ga.	4ga.	4ga.	4ga.
65-85A	6ga.	6ga.	4ga.	4ga.	2ga.	2ga.
85-105A	6ga.	6ga.	4ga.	2ga.	2ga.	2ga.
105-125A	4ga.	4ga.	4ga.	2ga.	2ga.	0ga.
125-150A	2ga.	2ga.	2ga.	2ga.	0ga.	0ga.

Wire size chart from the IASCA handbook. The size of wire used in any circuit is determined by the current load and the length of the wire. This chart is for copper wire (don't use aluminum wire).

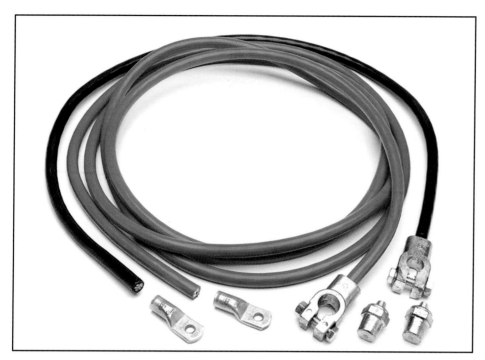

As the battery gets farther away from the starter, the cables must be a heavier gauge. These one-gauge, fine-strand cables from Painless are extra long for trunk mounted batteries.

Fuses and terminals are color coded to their intended use and optimum current load.

from being forced off the bench. Resistance is measured in ohms.

The way these three forces interact is contained in a very simple formula known as Ohm's Law.

Ohm's Law: V = IxR or stated another way, I =V/R and R=V/I

To take our earlier example just a little farther, consider that at the end of the bench there's a turnstile and the people going through the turnstile are like current causing an electric motor to rotate. We also need to consider the size of the bench. The bench (which represents the wire) is only intended to hold so many people. If it has too many people on it, it could collapse.

THE IMPORTANCE OF WIRE SIZE

The size of wire is very important in the flow of electrons. The larger the wire, with more strands in the wire, the more current it can carry. To relate this to the park bench think of a sport facility where there are rows of benches. Each bench represents one strand of wire, the more strands the more flow. Even though the benches may not always be full of people the potential is there if needed.

Different wire sizes and types are manufactured with different amounts of strands. Most household wire is made of a single heavy strand, good for carrying high voltages and low current. In the automotive applications the wire is sized from light to heavy and is always made up of many strands, which is good for carrying higher current flows at relatively low voltage. Multiple strands also makes the wire flexible and less prone to breakage from vibration.

The size of a wire is known as its gauge. Bigger numbers indicate a smaller wire able to carry a smaller current. A 22 gauge wire might be used for a dash circuit, while a 2 or 4 gauge wire would make a good battery cable.

Even within a given gauge, different types of wires will have different numbers of strands. Higher quantity wire generally contains a larger number of smaller diameter strands.

As a general rule of thumb, always use the highest number of strands per wire size as possible. A good example of this is battery cable. Many people use welding cable for their battery cables because it has much higher stranding than regular battery cable. This results in less voltage drop and heat build up during use, due to the lower resistance of the multiple strands.

This TXL wire from Painless uses a very high quality, high temperature insulation that is actually thinner than the insulation on the hardware-store wire most of us are familiar with.

WIRE SIZE IN A CIRCUIT

Charts are available that give the recommended gauge size for a particular situation (see the wire size chart). The two things that determine the gauge needed for a circuit are the current load the wire will need to carry, and the length of the wire that carries that load. More current requires a larger diameter wire (smaller gauge number). The same current, but in a longer piece of wire, will require a larger diameter wire. When in doubt, go larger, not smaller.

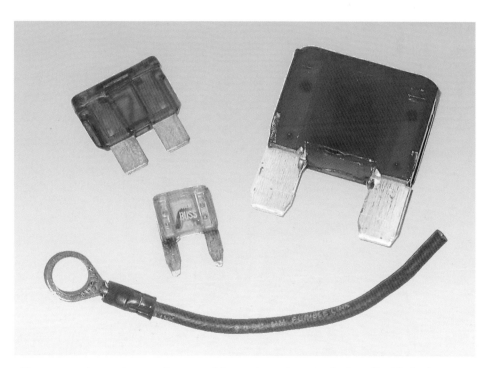

Fuses come in various ratings, and in various sizes, including fusible links.

FAQ: Dennis Overholser

Dennis Overholser is the driving force behind all the products in the Painless Wiring catalog. His training in electronics started in the military, extended through his years as a professional mechanic, and continues to this day with his day-to-day involvement with all aspects of street rodding. Dennis has plenty to say about what makes a good wiring harness and how to re-wire your car or truck with a minimum of time and trouble.

What makes a good wiring harness or harness kit?

Number one, it has to be complete. There are so many times when you go buy something, especially in the street rod market - you go buy

More at home in a shop than an office, Dennis Overholser is the man responsible for the design of all Painless Products.

it and it's not all there. You may need some nuts and bolts, or whatever it is, to put it together. My goal is that when you open the box, you don't have to go and buy anything else. Nothing else required. You need a few tools, of course, like everything else. But everything is there, all the terminals and everything you need.

The second thing that I look at - there are a lot of different versions of wiring kits out on the market today - and almost everyone does it differently. The majority of the kits start at the fuse block or fuse panel or whatever they want to call it. They tell you to mount it and then attach the wires at the end, like at the headlight or the taillight, and run all the wires back to the fuse panel which then becomes a junction block.

Well, we do it a little bit differently. And the reason I do it differently is because number one, up underneath the dash is the hardest place to get to. The seat is in the way, the brake pedal is in the way. So why spend all of the time up underneath the dash? Spend the least amount of time underneath the dash. Let's pre-do all the connections at the fuse block, stick it up underneath the dash, mount it properly, and then run the wires out from there. Once it's mounted, you're physically done. No standing on your head, no removing the seat, no cursing the brake pedal. Then you lay the wires out the way you like them, cut off the excess and terminate them. To me, that's a lot simpler.

The biggest enemy to electrical wiring is bad connections. At Painless we make as many of the connections as possible in the factory. The crimps are made by machines and checked with micrometers to be sure they are

FAQ: Dennis Overholser

squeezed just hard enough and not too hard. Then we know all the connections at the fuse box are going to be okay. The customer doesn't have to worry about that. And it saves a tremendous amount of questions on the tech line. We don't have to worry about whether or not they hooked the headlight wire to the right terminal on the fuse box.

Are there differences in terms of the quality of the components used in the various wiring kits?

Well, there are some industry standards for components, although different quality kits are available. We get the highest quality components that we can and we strive to have everything American made, because that's what people want. The big difference, I guess, is in the wire.

There are lots of different kinds of wire on the market. If you go down to a local auto supply, you'd get what we call GPT. It's just general purpose wire. For years, we used UL 1015. It's a higher-grade, lower-temperature wire with really heavy insulation, its excellent wire.

Today, all our wire is TXL. TXL has a very high temperature rating on the insulation, 125 degrees centigrade. The insulation is a lot thinner so it's lighter weight and less bulky. This is what the big three are currently using, and all the people that we do business with at NASCAR want TXL because it's lighter weight. So we have totally converted over everything that we do to TXL, you can't buy higher quality automotive wire.

Painless uses TXL wire in all their harnesses. The wire is shipped in barrels which contain up to 55,000 feet.

FAQ: Dennis Overholser

When people wire a car, and it's a whole re-wire, what are the typical mistakes they make?

The biggest mistake that most people make is they don't read the instructions. I'm going to say 99 times out of 100 if they read the instructions, they wouldn't be calling us on the tech line. The reason that a lot of people don't read the instructions is because they think they already know how to do the wiring. They've already wired some cars in the past and they think, 'I already know what I'm doing, I don't need to read these.' They probably don't realize that we spend a tremendous amount of time doing the drawings and providing information in the instruction books. That's probably the biggest problem that we have.

As far as any problems that happen, sometimes people get confused. In the past they may take the bundle out of the box, and they take off some of the informational tags that are on the wires and now they're kind of lost and they're not sure where one or two wires go. Now we print the destination of each wire on the entire length to assure proper routing.

With fuel injection kits, which we do a tremendous amount of, the questions never end. The biggest problem with that is most people don't understand the basics of fuel injection, why it works, how it works, and what it was designed to do. They may have a problem and because they don't understand it, or they don't know what's going on, they don't have a clue as to how to troubleshoot it. They don't even know where to start. Over the years we've compiled all these questions we get on fuel injection and put the questions and answers into our instruction book. And we try to do it in layman's terms. But still somebody gets confused because a fuel injection harness is very complex. But as far as the number one cause of problems, that would probably be from not reading the instructions.

So there's no reason a reasonably competent individual can't install either a wiring kit or an EFI kit?

That's right. The whole idea is to design the kits so, especially the EFI kits, everything is a plug in. With the fuel injection kits, if there's a wire that does not have a terminal already on the end, and a good example is a fuel pump wire, the only reason it doesn't is because we don't know how long to make that wire because we don't know where that customer has mounted the fuel pump. So he stretches the wire out, gets it where it should

Among the EFI harness kits available from Painless is this 60102 designed for 1986-89 TPI 5.0L and 5.7L V8 engines using a MAF sensor or Mass Air Flow system. GM computer chip or VATS module may be required.

FAQ: Dennis Overholser

be, cuts off the excess and then terminates it. All the injectors, all the sensors, the computer, everything has a connector. If it's possible, we go ahead and pre-terminate the end.

That's a little unlike our regular harness because the only thing we pre-terminate on our main harnesses are the terminals for the fuse block and some of the switches. But as far as the light switch connections to the headlights and taillights and turn signals, we don't know if it's going to be an Isetta that's six feet long or if it's going to be a '42 Cadillac that's 19 feet long. We provide plenty of wire and leave it up to the customer to lay out the wires, cut off the excess and install terminals.

Do you have tips for a typical harness install?

The first thing I tell the customer, if it's a rewire job, 'take all of the old wiring out of the vehicle.' That's the best thing to do unless there is a small harness that is to be re-used, such as a wiper-motor harness. Making notes of some special connections and routing. The reason we recommend this is because it avoids confusion. You've got a couple of old wires hanging down that they didn't take out and then they want to tie them in and they wonder, do I tie it in here or there?' If there's nothing in there, there's no question about what wire goes where or how to tie it together. So that's the first thing. Get everything stripped out and get it clean, then start from scratch. Mount the fuse block, and run the three groups of wire: one group goes to the front, one group to the dash, the other group goes to the tail section - it's just that simple. Lay them out the way you want, cut off the excess, and install terminals.

Do you like to see wires soldered or not? For example, what about the wires I run up to the headlight group and the headlights themselves?

I have nothing against soldering wires. In fact, there are two ways to look at it. Number one, if you were building a television set that's going to be sitting there in your living room and not moving around and not vibrating, there's only one way to go, that's solder everything. In an automobile, it's a different situation. The big factor in soldering in cars is, who does the soldering? A factory trained person or someone who's never soldered before?

Take an average Joe on the street who probably has a soldering iron in his hand once or twice a year, at best, the first thing he's going to do is overheat the terminal. He may not know how to make solder flow. When he doesn't know how to make the solder flow, then he overheats everything and the wire tends to crystallize. Once the wire crystallizes it takes just very little flex, and the wire breaks so it didn't do any good to solder it. So in the average installation we highly recommend just using crimp terminals. You can crimp one and the odds are it's not going to break, and the crimp does have a little bit of strain relief built into it. That's why they're a little bit longer than they actually need to be. For everyday use, use a good quality crimp terminal and tool but if you're a professional and you use a soldering iron everyday in your work or whatever and you know the proper way to do things, that's great. Solder and heat shrink works great. Otherwise people should use a crimp connector. That's why we provide good high-quality crimp connectors in all of our kits.

You said a lot of people have trouble with grounds and relays. Can you explain?

One of the questions we get is, when I turn on the light switch or the turn signals, the instruments tend to go crazy. This is a very common problem and usually it's caused by a bad ground. The indicator light that's trying to operate in the dash has a bad ground, so it grounds through something else that does have a good ground, like the gauges.

FAQ: Dennis Overholser

The other problem is that people don't ground the body. Let's say you put your battery in the trunk and run the battery cable down to the frame and bolt it on there. That's wonderful but people forget to tie the body and engine to the frame. The engine can't ground through the motor mounts and the body's sitting on rubber pads. You have to run a ground strap or cable between the battery, frame and engine, and at least a ten gauge wire grounding the body. Good grounds like this will prevent a tremendous number of problems.

The second most common problem area involves the use of relays to power high current devices such as electric fans, air conditioning systems, electric fuel pumps, or anything that's going to be a real high current draw item (more on relays in Chapter Five). If you try to supply all the power necessary to operate those devices through the fuse block, what sometimes happens is you're trying to consume more than the fuse block, and the internal circuitry of the fuse block, can handle. Sometimes you get a tremendous voltage drop. If you check one of the affected circuits with a volt meter, you'll notice that the reading went from 13.2 to 10.1 or 9.8 volts.

Then most people figure the charging system is not working, but that's not necessarily the case. The charging system may be doing just wonderful supplying power to the battery, but the internal circuitry or fuse block is not capable of handling all the amperage necessary to fulfill the needs of the devices drawing current through the fuse block. What we do then is add a relay. A relay is a simple electronically controlled switch. The power that would normally go through a key switch or through a toggle switch is now transmitted through the relay. We take power directly from the battery source; through the relay to the cooling fan or fuel

pump or whatever. The relay is turned on and off by a remote switch.

By using the relay you eliminate the voltage drop. A big part of the current load is taken off the fuse block. The customer can see that the charging system is working fine and probably was working fine all along.

If I've got an old car, like pre-1956, and I want to keep some of the 6 volt components, the gauges maybe, what's the easiest way to do that?

Gauges and radios require a fixed voltage. The only way you can do that is by way of an electronic voltage regulator. There are a couple different ones being made on the market (Painless discontinued the manufacture of these units). Usually they consist of a simple solid state circuit and a heat sink. What we're doing is bringing in 12 volts, grounding out 6 of the volts and allowing 6 of the volts to continue out. A lot of people have tried using ceramic-type resistors to cut the voltage down, but they won't work because a resistor cuts down voltage by heat, and it takes a lot of current flow to pro-

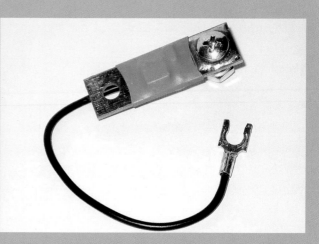

The Runtz, offered by Fifth Avenue Antique Auto Parts, attaches directly to the input terminal of the 6 volt gauge. 12 volts can then be applied to the Runtz and it will step the voltage down for safe gauge operation.

FAQ: Dennis Overholser

duce enough heat to increase the resistance enough to cut the current flow down. Similar to an ignition resistor, they get extremely hot and they work great, because they're pulling 5, maybe 10, amps no problem. You take a gauge or series of gauges that are pulling milliamps, the resistor will never pull enough current to get hot and to make the resistance needed to drop the current flow. So you can't do it. That's why the electronic style voltage converter is the only way you can do it. They work great. A lot of people use them. The only downfall to these is the current output. Most of them are only rated to 5 amps, so you can run the gauges and the radio fine, but if you want to run the wiper motor or a heater motor then you have to go back to the ceramic resistor.

Are there any tips you want to pass on before they jump out there and do their first rewiring job?

The number one thing you have to have to do a wiring job is patience. If you can read, understand drawings, understand color codes,

that's all great but the key is having the patience to sit down and not get in a hurry. Don't say, 'I'm just going to go ahead and run this wire over here because I want to hear it run,' and forget about the rest of the car. The first thing you know, you have that wire and all the other wires going in different directions, and you think, 'I wish I'd have waited because now my wires are too short.'

There's a lot of redundancy in a wiring job. You're going back over the same group of wires four or five times. Run a wire, crimp a terminal, run a wire, crimp a terminal. It gets boring. It's not near as much fun as bolting on a set of billet wheels. But if you don't do it right the first time you're stuck on the side of the road. Patience! Follow the instructions. It's amazing the number of people who call in and say, 'I've never done one before, I did it and it started the first time.'

It was supposed to start the first time. It's simple, and a lot of people try to make it harder than it actually is.

When it comes to wiring, neatness definitely counts. Protect and clean up any harness installation with this braided wire wrap. The laterally split design closes around wire bundle without the need for additional taping or fasteners. Available in 4 diameters. Painless

The other thing to consider when buying wire is the quality of the insulation. At Painless Wiring we use TXL, with insulation that is thinner, yet more heat and abrasion resistant than anything else on the market.

Remember that the new high temperature insulation, like that used with TXL,, are thinner than the insulation used with lesser grades of wire making it hard to gauge the gauge of the wire. What looks at first like a 16 gauge wire might actually be 14 gauge wire with the new, thinner insulation.

CIRCUIT PROTECTION DEVICES

Fuses

A fuse is one of the most important parts of the electrical circuit. The fuse is the weak link in the passage of current and is designed to allow only a preset amount of current to flow through the circuit. By using a fuse, regulation of current flow is possible, and damage to sensitive electronic parts and powered circuits can be avoided. A fuse works by having a small conductive strip between the two contacts that is designed to melt at a certain temperature. When current flow reaches a certain maximum level, the natural resistance of the strip creates enough heat to melt the strip, thus stopping current flow. If a wire rubs through the insulation and contacts the frame, the fuse will blow well before the wire gets hot enough to melt. Without a fuse you run the risk of melting the wires in one or more circuits and starting a fire in the car.

Fusible links

A fusible link as used by the factory is a short link of melt-able wire housed in high temperature insulation. Generally used to carry a load heavier than a standard fuse can handle, fusible links are again the weak link in a chain, designed to melt before the wire or circuit itself are damaged. Detroit often uses a fusible link where a large feed wire (eight or ten gauge) connects to the starter solenoid or source of battery power. If the wire with the fusible link in it shorts to ground someplace "down stream" the link will melt, preventing the entire wire from burning up.

Diodes

A diode is simply an electronic one-way valve, passing current one way and one way only. The most common use of diodes is in an alternator, where two banks of diodes are used to convert alternating current to direct current.

Basic headlight circuit uses a circuit breaker to protect the headlights while a fuse or fuses protect the tail and parking lights.

Current flow in a diode is always in the direction of the band at one end of its body. The band will sometimes have an arrow pointing to it which shows current flow direction. The banded end is the exit for current.

RESISTORS

Resistors are current restrictor devices sometimes used to add a load to a circuit or to reduce the voltage in a circuit. Resistors can be made of carbon, ceramic or a combination of electronic items when making a constant output voltage reducer.

Carbon, ceramic, and other types of traditional resistors are normally used to reduce a circuit voltage by a certain percentage and may come in any size. The small carbon resistor shown comes with color coded rings around it which indicates its resistance and wattage capacity. These resistors usually will not carry a large amount of current, but are more precise in their capabilities to reduce voltage. An ignition resistor, for instance, used in earlier point type distributors, reduces the input voltage to help reduce arcing of the point contacts which in turn aids in prolonging point life. Its typical voltage drop would be from 12 volts down to about 9 volts. Some ceramic resistors may be connected in series to further reduce the voltage. An example might be a 6 volt heater motor in a vehicle that has been converted to 12 volts.

NOTE: These large ceramic resistors get very hot and can damage paint, wiring, or interior compo-

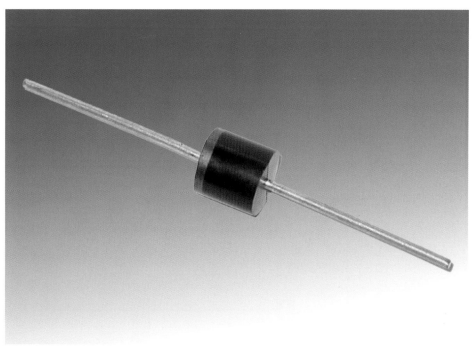

Diodes are a one way valve for electrical current. The silver ring on one end indicates the outlet side of current flow.

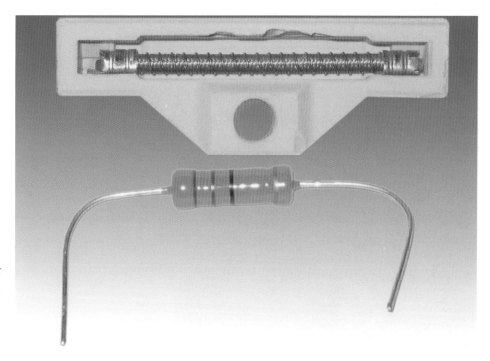

The ceramic resistor on top is often used to drop voltage for motors and other high current usage devices. The typical carbon resistor (lower image) with the colored bands is used in computer circuitry and where resistance is required to control voltage.

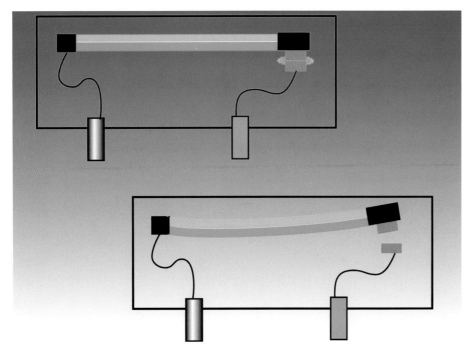

Too much current moving through the bi-metallic strip in this auto-reset circuit breaker creates heat, which causes the dis-similar metals to expand at different rates - and open the circuit.

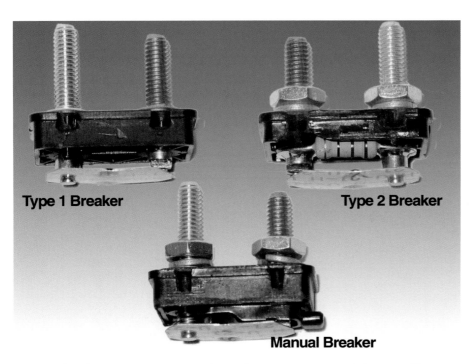

Type 1 Breaker

Type 2 Breaker

Manual Breaker

Circuit breakers come in many styles and amperage ratings. Type 1 will automatically reset as will the type 2 when the short has been repaired. The manual will reset when the button on the end is depressed.

nents. Always mount them where they will have good air flow.

Electronic voltage reducers are usually built to control a specific device. The most common use in hot rods is to control the voltage to the gauges. Many cars and trucks today are still running with the original 6 volt gauges and the use of an electronic reducer will allow 12 volts to be stepped down to 6 volts for gauge operation. Unlike larger ceramic resistors, an electronic voltage reducer (resistor) will not carry a high amperage load. Some are made to control up to 5 amps and small ones like the one shown are designed to operate only one gauge.

Circuit Breakers

Circuit breakers, like fuses, are designed to protect circuits from overloading. The major difference between fuses and circuit breakers is that fuses, when overloaded, melt the conductive strip and are not reusable. Circuit breakers, by contrast, have a bimetallic strip that heats up under overload conditions causing a break in the current flow. There are three basic types of circuit breakers being used in automobiles.

Type 1 automatic reset

This type of circuit breaker will automatically reset itself when the bimetallic strip cools. This is the most commonly used type and will continue to turn current off and on as long as the circuit is overloaded. In some type circuits this could be dangerous and damage electronic devices. In a headlight circuit, however, a driver wants the circuit breaker to reset as quickly as possible so the lights are turned back on.

Type 2 automatic reset

This type of circuit will automatically reset only when the overload is removed from the circuit. The bimetallic strip breaks contact like the type 1, but there is a small special resistor along side of the strip which is attached to the contacts. Current passes through this resistor when the main contacts have opened. The heat of the resistor prevents the bimetallic strip from cooling and remaking contact. This type circuit breaker is becoming the preferred choice for electrical system designers because of the higher safety factor.

Manual reset

The manual reset circuit breaker also has the bimetallic strip but it will not reset itself when cooled. The strip is pushed back into place, usually with an external button on the circuit breaker housing, and contact of the circuit is remade. This type is most commonly used in electric motors and circuits that have high voltages such as your home or workshop

CONTROL DEVICES

Relays

A relay can be thought of as a remote switch controlled by another switch. The relay is designed to pass relatively large amounts of current to specific devices, rather than have that current pass through switches and major harnesses. Relays are often used to prevent overloading of circuits, switches and fuse blocks. Simple relays commonly have two circuits, a load circuit that actually carries the heavy load from the battery to the electric fan or pump, and a control circuit that is used to switch the load circuit on and off.

Relays are usually mounted remotely and close to the device that is requiring the extra high current. Power is transferred directly from the battery source to the device through the relay that has been turned on by a switch. In most cases, relays are protected by circuit breakers from overloading.

In a typical hot rod application two different relays are used. Most automotive relays have a single input from the battery source and one or two outputs to the load.

A. Single pole single throw (SPST). The pole is the number of output contacts activated by the magnetic coil internally. The throw is the number of directions the internal contacts travel internally to allow current to flow. These relays will pass current only when activated The output may be a single terminal to operate a horn or split internally in the relay and have two external terminals of which to attach wires. An application may be routing separate wires to two small cooling fans.

B. Single pole double throw (SPDT). This style of relay will pass current to one output post when activated and to a different output post when deactivated or sometimes called "at rest". This style relay is often used in lighting and separation of circuits like integrated brake and turn signals. The two output terminals usually have different current carrying capacities, due to internal workings, as shown by the relay on the right in the photo.

A good example of a relay would be a horn cir-

Although a lot more expensive, blade style circuit breakers that are designed to plug in where an ATO style fuse would go are convenient in certain applications.

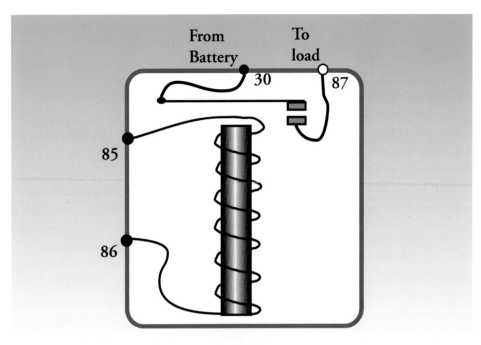

From Battery

To load

30

87

85

86

This schematic shows the internal workings of a basic 4-prong electric relay. A small current moving between 85 and 86 (the control side of the relay) creates a magnetic field which closes the load carrying part of the relay.

Cube relays, like the one on the left, are the most popular and versatile. The mini-breaker on the right is handy in tight spots but is limited in current carrying capacity.

cuit. When you hit the horn button you're usually grounding the control circuit in the relay, which causes the load side of the relay to close allowing current to flow from the battery to the horn. By using a relay there is no need to run the heavy wires needed to power the horn up to, and through, the steering column.

Solenoids

Solenoids are sometimes referred to as large relays. They come in many sizes and configurations. The ones most common in the hot rod industry are used on starter motors or battery kill switch kits.

A solenoid used in a starter circuit is really nothing more than a specialized relay. In the case of a stand-alone solenoid mounted to the fender or firewall, the solenoid is activated by the ignition switch. When the switch is turned to the start position, battery voltage is applied to the coil in the solenoid.

Inside the coil is a movable plunger with a copper disc attached to one end. When the coil is energized, a magnetic field causes the plunger to overcome spring pressure and be drawn into the coil. As this happens the copper disc is brought into contact with two terminals inside the solenoid. One of these terminals is connected to the battery, the other connects to the starter.

In the case of a solenoid attached to the starter, the plunger has an additional task. In addition to moving the copper disc up against the two larger terminals it also moves the starter drive gear into mesh with the flywheel.

Many starter solenoids include a second small terminal that is only energized when the starter is activated, and can be used as a by-pass for an ignition resistor. Check chapter 2 for more on starter circuits.

A battery kill solenoid is usually connected in series with the positive battery cable. When the solenoid is activated it will allow current to flow through the cable. When shut off the battery is then isolated from the rest of the electrical system.

There are two styles of these solenoids. Latching and non-latching.

Latching solenoids have a device internally that holds the contacts either open or closed until the magnetic plunger moves to trip it. These require only a momentary current to activate. The positive thing about this style solenoid is there is no battery drain when the vehicle is in storage or not in use. The negative thing is the maximum amount of constant current flow is about 100 amps.

Non-latching solenoids require a constant current to hold the internal contacts together. The positive thing about these solenoids is the large amount of continuous current, about 250 amps, they will carry. The negative thing about this style solenoid is that if left on for long periods of time the battery will drain.

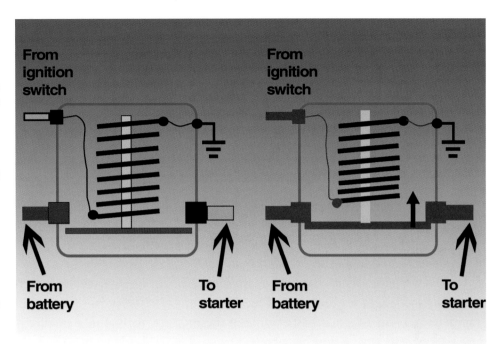

A typical solenoid is nothing more than a specialized relay. When you turn the key the control circuit is energized, which pulls the big copper disc upward until it connects the two load terminals, delivering power from the battery to the starter.

Solenoids like the ones shown are high amperage capacity relays. The one on the left is a latching solenoid used for battery disconnects and will carry in the range of 125 amps continuously. The solenoid in the center, rated at 250 amps, continuous is often used for controlling multiple battery applications. The Ford style solenoid on the right is most commonly used for engine starter activation.

Chapter Two

Batteries, Starters, Alternators

Heart and Soul of the System

Like everything else, the world of batteries, starters and alternators is changing as we speak. New battery designs are announced by the major manufacturers on a regular basis. Some of these new energy cells have a number of advantages, especially for a hot rod or specialized vehicle.

Starters and alternators are evolving too. On the starter front, the mini starter offers more torque in a smaller package than anything offered by Detroit. Alternators have gone from the 40 or

At the heart of your electrical system is the battery, a device that both creates and stores electricity. To keep the battery charged and healthy you need an alternator, one with enough output to answer the needs of your electrical system.

50 amp models many of us grew up with, to standard outputs of well over 100 amps. High output and aftermarket examples are now available with outputs of double that figure.

This chapter is intended to give you an introduction to the ways in which each component: battery, starter, and alternator operate, as well as pictures and illustrations to show how to install them in your hot rod. With more understanding of how each component operates you are in a better position to buy something appropriate for your individual needs and install it correctly.

BATTERIES

The heart of any vehicle electrical system is the battery, not only a power source, but also a regulator of voltage in the electrical system. The battery in your car serves three major functions.

The battery is an electricity producing device. The chemical reaction between the lead plates and the electrolyte, a water and sulfuric acid mix, creates electrical current. The voltage is determined by the number of cells.

The battery is also a storage device. The battery can store a large amount of current in its plates and is capable of providing this current to the electrical system on demand.

The battery is also a regulator of current in the sys-

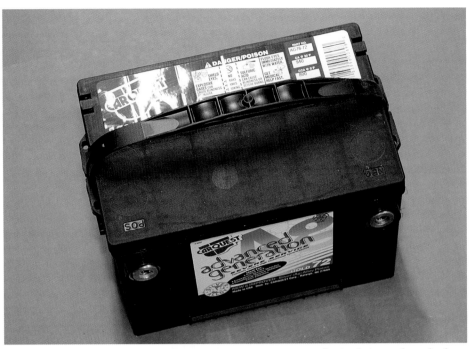

Batteries come in various physical sizes, though the Group 24 (shown) is the most common. Batteries also come with top and side posts. Side posts are handy if there's very little clearance on top of the battery. And though this is a no maintenance design, it isn't actually sealed.

Batteries are rated by their expected longevity, the cold cranking amps and reserve capacity. This is a typical starter battery, meaning it's designed to put out a lot of power for starting, then be recharged quickly by the alternator.

tem. As the engine rpm or system loads increase or decrease, the voltage and current flow go up and down. The battery acts as a buffer to dampen spikes and stabilize voltage in the system.

There are two basic configurations for automotive batteries: top-post and side-post. The top-post style has been around forever. The two lead posts are tapered, typically the positive post is slightly larger in diameter than the negative post.

The side-post battery was developed to help solve several problems. Because the posts are not next to the caps or vents, a source of acid fumes, corrosion of the terminals is reduced. The added benefit of the side post terminal location is the lowered silhouette which allows the batteries to fit more easily into modern cars with lowered hood lines.

Batteries carry a number of ratings, the two most common include cold cranking amps and reserve capacity. Cold cranking amps is the amount of current the battery can provide for a certain length of time at a given temperature. To determine the rating, a battery is chilled to 0° F and placed under a load in amps for 30 seconds while maintaining a voltage of 7.2 volts. The larger the rating number, such as 500/600/750, the more power that battery can put out to start your vehicle.

The reserve capacity rating is a means of determining how long a battery might supply current in a situation where the charging circuit has failed. This is the length of time, in minutes, that a fully charged battery can be discharged at 25 amps without allowing the individual cell voltage to drop below 1.75 volts.

BATTERY BASICS
Construction

Automotive batteries are constructed of posi-

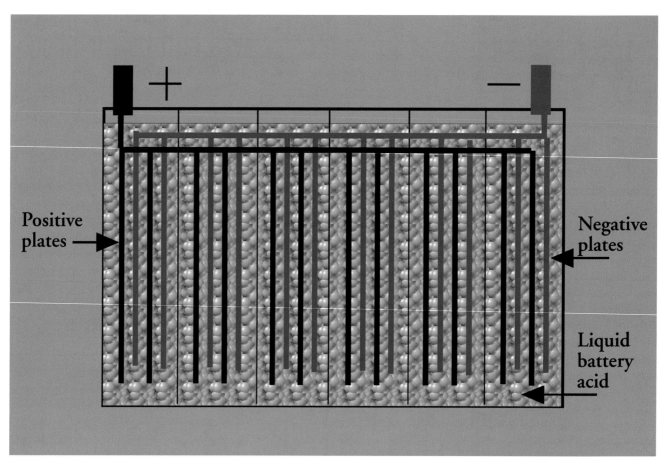

Typical wet-cell batteries group alternating negative and positive plates in 6 cells, each capable of producing 2 volts.

tive and negative plates kept apart by separators, grouped into cells, connected by straps and suspended in a solution of electrolyte. Though standard wisdom would suggest batteries with longer warranties are built with more plates, a Delco engineer explained that the situation is more complex than that. Batteries with the longest warranties actually have a plate of a slightly different type than a battery with a shorter warranty, and the plates themselves might actually be thicker so fewer of them could fit into the battery case. Each cell of the battery produces approximately two volts, by connecting six cells in series a 12 volt battery is created.

SAFETY WARNING

Nearly all batteries emit hydrogen gas, explosive to say the least. Gassing is especially likely when the battery is being charged by an external charger but also when the battery is under a load. For these reasons, cigarettes, sparks and flames must be kept away from the battery. When jump starting a car be sure the last connection to be made is the negative cable, connected to the frame or engine block of the car being jumped. That way any spark occurs away from the battery.

Wrenches laid on the battery have a potential to short across the terminals

The Optima, one of the more common of new battery designs on the market, is a truly sealed battery using spiral-wound plates that are locked in place and thus less prone to damage from vibration.

Available in both red, and yellow-top designs, the red-top battery is designed for starting. Note the battery's specifications on the top.

and create an explosion. Also remember that metal jewelry conducts electricity at least as well as a wrench (silver and gold are both excellent conductors), which is one more reason to take off the watch and rings before you start work on the hot rod. Remember too that batteries contain sulfuric acid, corrosive to metal and damaging to human skin. Spilled acid should be flushed thoroughly with water.

BATTERY CHEMISTRY

The plates of the battery are made of lead alloys. Specifically the positive plates are made of lead peroxide while the negative plates are made of sponge lead. These plates are suspended in a solution made up of sulfuric acid and water. When the battery discharges, sulfate (sulfur and oxygen) from the electrolyte combines with the lead on both the positive and negative plates.

As these sulfur compounds are bound to the lead plates oxygen is released from the positive plates. The oxygen mixes with hydrogen in the electrolyte to form water. As this reaction continues the acid becomes weaker and weaker, and more and more sulfate coats the plates. Charging the battery reverses the chemical process, forcing sulfates back into solution with the electrolyte and causing oxygen from the solution to move back onto the positive plates.

The down side to all this charging and discharging business is the inevitable flaking of lead particles off the plates until the battery's ability to act as a battery is greatly diminished. Further affecting battery performance is the fact that sulfates penetrate too deeply into the lead plates to be driven back into solution, creating the condition often referred to as "sulfated."

Specific gravity is often used to check the state of charge for non-sealed batteries. Specific

Jewelry, such as rings and watches, and keys, all are conductors of electricity. Removal of jewelry is a must because severe injury can result from just a second of contact with a battery source.

gravity simply measures the weight of a liquid as compared to water. The specific gravity of a fully charged battery (with strongly acidic electrolyte) ranges from 1.260 to 1.280 at 80° F or 1.260 to 1.280 times as heavy as the same volume of water. As the battery becomes discharged the specific gravity drops because the electrolyte has a higher percentage of water. This is also why a discharged battery will freeze on a cold winter's night while a fully charged battery will not.

Low and no-maintenance batteries change the chemical and physical construction of the plates slightly. By adding a chemical like calcium to the plates and changing the structure of the plates themselves, gassing of the battery is greatly reduced. This means a much smaller volume of corrosive/explosive gasses, little or no loss of water, and generally improved performance.

Recombination batteries, sometimes known under the name valve-regulated, go even further. These batteries contain all the "electrolyte" in a porous glass mat positioned between the cells. There is no liquid acid in batteries of this type and they can be mounted in nearly any position. As a General Motors (GM) engineer explained, "the chemistry is the same as a conventional

Take seriously the warning panels on the top of most batteries, they can explode. Be especially careful when connecting or disconnecting cables after charging or jumping from another battery. Any spark can ignite the hydrogen gas and give you a face full of acid.

The only battery chargers that can stay connected to a battery long-term, and not create too much heat, are the "smart" designs like the Battery Tender shown here (and available in various capacities).

lead-acid battery, but the hydrogen and oxygen can move back and forth from the plates to the glass mats without the gassing you see in a standard 'flooded' battery design."

Sometimes confused with recombination batteries, the new gel-cell batteries are quite different internally. Though they are often used for golf carts or stationary applications these designs are currently not suitable for automotive applications because they are so easily damaged during recharging.

DEEP CYCLE BATTERIES

Golf cart batteries are known as deep-cycle, meaning they are designed from the beginning to be discharged to less than half their capacity with no ill effects. A standard automotive battery, on the other hand, is designed to put out a relatively short burst of high-amperage power, to start the car, and then be quickly recharged by the alternator. Using an automotive battery in a deep cycle application will shorten its life considerably.

KEEP IT CHARGED FOR LONG LIFE

All batteries self discharge to some extent. This means a fully charged battery will draw itself to zero voltage over time, even if the battery cables are removed. The answer is to recharge the battery when the vehicle sits for any extended period of time. This becomes doubly important with the new fuel injection and radio designs which place a small load (but still a load) on the battery at all times. Don't allow the battery to run down and don't let it sit for any length of time in a discharged condition.

Other tips for long life are mostly common sense. Keep the battery clean because a film of acid and dirt will conduct a small current between the terminals, speeding the self discharge.

BATTERY MOUNTING BASICS

Batteries, with the exception of the truly sealed recombinant designs, emit gasses that are very corrosive and explosive. When mounting any battery be sure to keep it away from high heat areas like exhaust pipes and manifolds. It's also necessary to keep the battery away from any source of sparks, such as the ignition system, that could accidentally ignite the gasses vented by most battery designs.

The closer the battery is to the starter the better it will perform in starting the engine. Different vehicles have larger or smaller areas to mount batteries in, often the battery for a hot rod is mounted in the trunk. In these situations it's good to remember that the farther the battery is from the starter, the larger the battery cables need to be in order to prevent

Mini starters pack two big advantage in a small package: increased torque to turn over big engines, and a small physical size providing clearance for headers and possibly the steering linkage. Tuff Stuff

excessive voltage drop. Though it's common practice to use the frame as the main conductor on the ground side of the battery-starter circuit, it's a better idea to run a ground cable from the battery's negative post to the engine. When using the frame, don't forget to connect the frame to the engine/transmission assembly with small ground straps made of battery cable or strap material. The engine, in most cases, is not directly connected to the chassis because of the rubber engine and transmission mounts.

The use of a steel or marine grade battery box to house the battery will protect the trunk from acid spills and also protect the battery case from damage due to items carried in the trunk. Some of the standard batteries use a vent tube, (Delco for example) which can be run through the floor if the battery is mounted in the trunk or interior of the car. Otherwise, the battery box itself must be vented to the outside, or the battery must be one of the truly sealed recombinant designs.

Battery cables are heavy so it is important to route the cables in a way that provides them with plenty of support. Running them inside the frame or solidly attached to the outside of the frame will prevent them from drooping and rubbing on a sharp frame edge or bracket. The last thing you want is for the cables to wear through their insulation, or contact the drive shaft or the exhaust system. Use plenty of brackets and ties to keep the cable(s) out of danger's way.

REMOTE BATTERY INSTALLATION

Keeping the engine compartment clean is sometimes a priority and to do so the battery is usually relocated. In a street rod or a classic the solution is simple, the trunk.

A steel battery box can protect against acid spills, as well as items in the trunk which could damage the battery case.

Mount Battery, Box & Cables

The battery box and cable kit are ready for installation. All required copper terminals, as well as simple instructions, are included.

The box is now mounted to the shelf.

Some left over hood welting is cut and glued to the bottom inside of the box to protect the battery from the mounting screws.

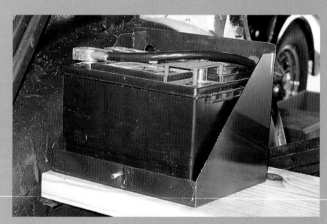

The shelf in place, the negative cable is routed through the floor and checked for proper length.

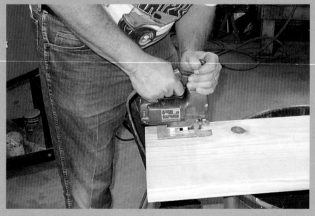

The shelf is measured and cut to size. A notch was also cut out to allow the cables to pass down to the floor openings.

A hammer style crimper is used to install a terminal on the negative cable. Crimp is (often) better than solder due to possible extreme heat of the starter.

Mount Battery, Box & Cables

The terminal now installed, a piece of heat shrink with glue inside is installed. The glue will protect the cable from moisture and corrosion.

The finished cable is routed and attached to the starter solenoid.

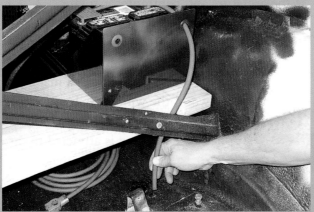

The positive cable is routed through the floor pan and down the frame rail.

A short piece of extra cable is terminated and covered to make a ground strap from tranny to frame. Star washers are used to make a good connection.

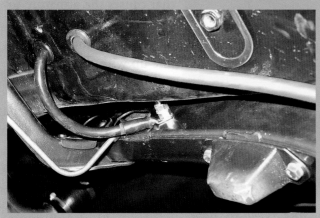

Rubber grommets are installed around the cables to prevent any future abrasion and possible shorts.

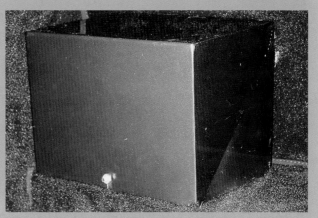

The finished installation. The cover installed protects the battery from articles placed in the trunk as well as making the battery attractive.

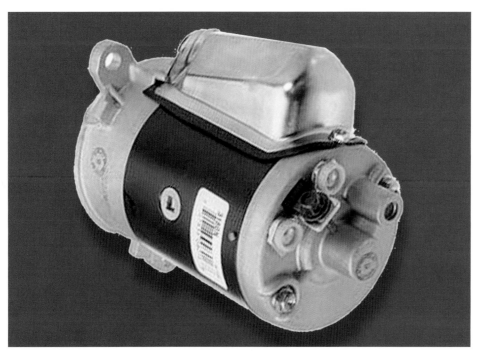

This Ford starter uses an external solenoid. When power is applied to the input post, the motor winding magnetic field pulls the plunger to activate the bendix.

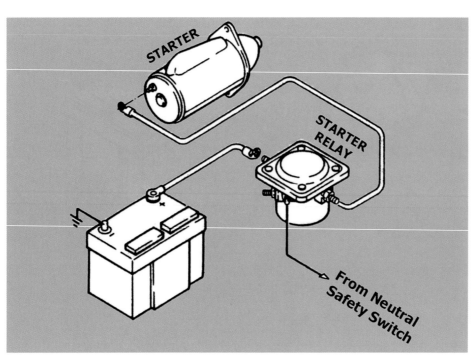

Typical Ford starter circuit. The other small terminal on the external solenoid is connected to the starter switch inside the car.

STARTER SOLENOIDS

Described briefly in Chapter One, starter solenoids are the switch between the starter and the battery.

Two main types of solenoids are used: the direct mount where the solenoid mounts directly on the starter (GM Style) and the remote mount, where the solenoid is mounted on the fender well or frame and a cable connects it to the starter (Ford Style). Both are good systems, though the direct mount solenoids are more likely to encounter hot-start problems due to heat build-up from the exhaust system.

Solenoid failure, or non-operation, is often due to excessive heat. As heat builds up so does resistance. The extra voltage and current required by the solenoid to overcome the resistance is, at times, not available because the battery cables are too small or the connections are dirty and corroded. Heat also creates expansion of the metals that the solenoid is constructed of. This expansion causes the plunger to drag in the case, increasing the current needed for activation.

A number of devices have been offered over the years to help owners overcome this hot start problem. The most common and useful is the kit made up primarily of a standard 30 amp relay that is located in the starter switch circuit. When the ignition switch is turned to start the relay is activated, and in turn transmits power from the battery terminal of the starter directly to the S-terminal on the solenoid. This is, in effect, a safe way of shorting the two terminals together with a screwdriver.

CHARGING SYSTEMS

The battery provides energy to start the car. Once it does start, that energy must, of course, be replaced. The charging system is designed to bring the battery back to a state of full charge and provide the power needed to run all the electrical systems on the vehicle.

Two different types of charging systems have been used in automobiles. Up until about 1960 most cars used a generator, while from that point on most cars relied on an alternator to keep the battery charged and provide energy for the vehicle electrical system.

A generator produces direct current voltage (DC), and uses a regulator to control the current and voltage output, and to connect the generator to the battery. Very early generators had only a cutout to control current to the battery. The higher the engine rpm the higher the voltage and current flow.

Alternators produce alternating current (AC), in which electrons flow first in one direction and then in the other. Since DC is used

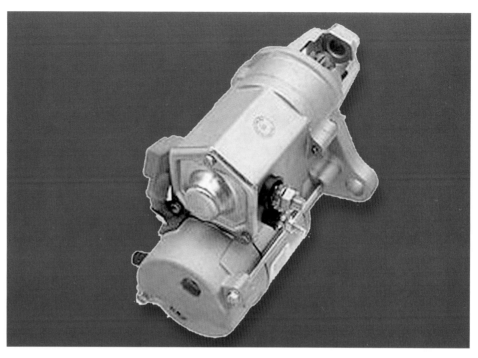

Chrysler starters have been gear-reduction style for many years. They operate in the same way as the GM style with the external solenoid. Now most manufacturers are using this style starter.

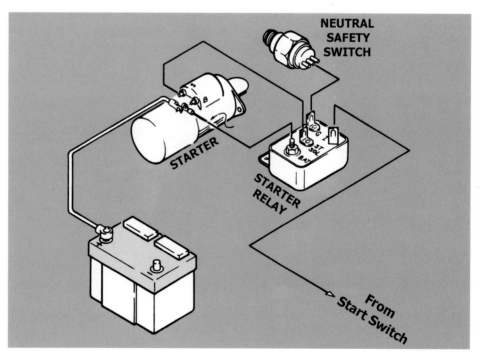

Typical Chrysler starter circuit. The neutral safely switch provides a ground (in P or N) which activates the relay which in turn delivers power to the starter solenoid windings.

The voltage regulator, the black plastic part with the blue dots, senses the voltage and current requirements of the electrical system and controls the alternator's output.

in automobiles, the AC current coming out of a raw alternator must be converted to DC. Diodes, often mounted in the alternator frame, convert the AC to DC electricity. Unlike generators, alternator current output is self regulating. Voltage, however, must be regulated. Though the first alternators used an external regulator for voltage, most alternators on late model automobiles use an internal voltage regulator.

Note: All alternator systems sense system voltage in order to determine the correct voltage output of the alternator. Thus, a bad battery will make it impossible for the alternator to work correctly and may also make testing of the alternator difficult. Because it's so important that the regulator sense the true condition of the charging system, it's very important that the alternator or generator, and any external regulator, be well grounded. If in doubt, use a star washer under the regulator base or a separate ground wire.

CONSTRUCTION DETAILS
Generators

DC generators are similar to starter motors in construction. The housing contains two field coils which create a magnetic field. Rotating inside the field coils is the armature wound with many windings. As these armature windings cut through the

Be careful, the G.M solenoids come in two lengths.

magnetic field created by the field windings a voltage is induced in the armature winding and fed to the commutator and then on to the brushes.

Because the field wires of a generator are wrapped around a permanent magnet, there is always some magnetic field for the armature windings to cut through. This is why you can push start an old car with a dead battery – the generator in the old '54 Chevy, with its permanent magnets, will "self excite" once it starts to turn. With a modern car, however, there must be some battery voltage before the alternator will produce energy.

Generators require a regulator to control current and voltage output. Most generator regulators are mechanical in design and use three sets of points, controlled by three corresponding coils of wire, to control voltage, current and the con-

nection between the generator and the battery.

Generators have a number of disadvantages when compared to alternators. Not only do they suffer generally lower total outputs, they need more RPM to produce power. If that weren't enough, generator brushes tend to wear relatively quickly as they ride on the segmented commutator.

GENERATOR TO ALTERNATOR CONVERSION
Alternators

Alternators were first used in mass produced automobiles in the early 1960s and have evolved into very sophisticated devices requiring minimal maintenance while producing power outputs undreamed of by generator designers.

Alternators contain the same basic components seen inside a generator, though the components are essentially reversed in position when compared to a generator. That is, the field wind-

Two G.M. solenoids and one Ford solenoid. The Ford starter connects the two small terminals to the ignition switch start position and the neutral safety switch.

The round black diodes are connected together to convert the alternating current (AC), produced by the alternator, to a direct current (DC) output.

ings are actually contained in the rotor, the component that spins, while the stator (which takes the place of the armature) is stationary and mounted to the alternator case. Because alternators produce alternating current (AC), two banks of diodes are used to convert this to direct current (DC).

Detroit switched from generators to alternators for good reason. Most alternators produce more power than a generator, and are able to provide a high percentage of that power at a relatively low speed. In addition, alternators will more readily spin to high rpm without damage. And though both generators and alternators contain brushes, the small alternator brushes run on the smooth slip rings of the rotor and thus last for a very long time.

Because factory alternators don't have a permanent magnet as part of their field windings, they will not self-excite. That is, no matter how fast you spin an alternator it will not produce power until the field is energized by an outside voltage source.

By adding permanent magnets, however, to a GM alternator, some aftermarket companies have created the "one wire" alternator. Because these units are internally regulated they need only one wire, the output wire

Slip rings located next to the outer bearing pass current through the brushes to the rotor windings. Magnetic fields then produce an output current. Note the internal cooling fan.

which typically runs to the battery. The "one wire" alternator has become very popular with hot rodders due to the ease of installation. The main disadvantage to these alternators is that a dash warning light may not be wired in and the use of a voltmeter or ammeter will be required. Also, most of these are based on earlier GM alternator designs so total output may not be as high as the more modern alternators.

Note: The large wire on the back of any alternator is hot all the time, thus many factory installations include an insulating cap of some type where the wire attaches to the alternator. Also note the output wire needs to be sized large enough to carry the full output of the alternator. In most cases this means at least an eight gauge wire.

HOW TO CHOOSE AN ALTERNATOR

One question that often comes up when building a car is: "How big an alternator do I need?"

In answer, remember that bigger is not always better. An alternator rated at 100 amps output will seldom put out more current than one rated at 65 amps. The output ratings are in direct relationship to the engine rpm. The larger, in size and output, alternators normally only have maximum outputs at the maximum rated rpm range.

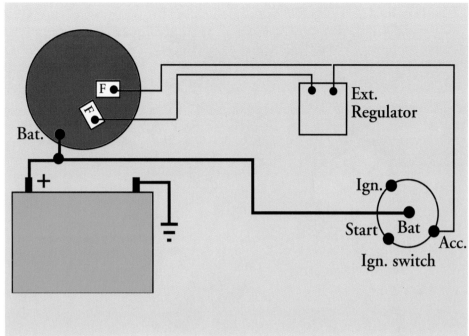

This early style Mopar alternator circuit uses the electronic, not mechanical, voltage regulator.

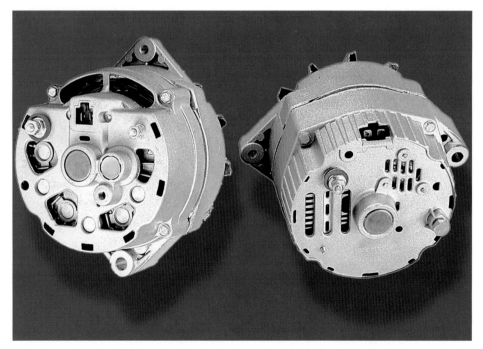

On the left, an early G.M alternator, which used an external regulator. On the right, a later model G.M. unit, with the regulator incorporated into the main unit. These newer alternators have much higher current outputs and use an ignition power wire to energize the regulator and allow charging.

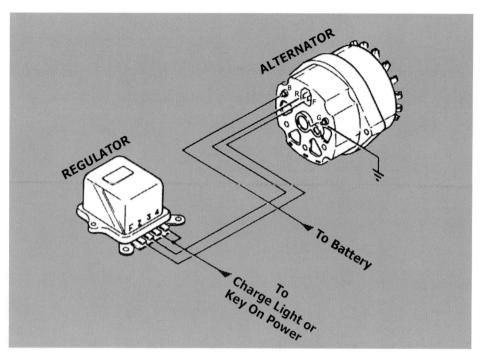

Early-style G.M. alternator and regulator circuit. When using this style be sure both the alternator and the regulator have a good ground.

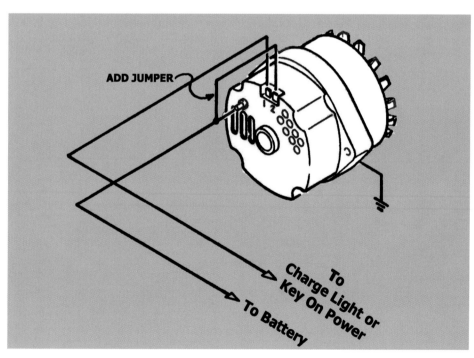

Delcotron style alternators are the most popular and easy to wire. Known as a three wire, they are used when an indicator light is required.

When choosing an alternator, determine first the amount of current needed by the system during full load conditions. The size of the alternator you choose should be close to that amount. Remember that it is very rare that all the circuits in a vehicle will be turned on at one time.

Plenty of hot rods are equipped with GM alternators simply because the drive train is likewise based on GM components. Among the newer GM alternators is the CS model, used on many GM products starting in about 1987. Smaller than the earlier alternators, these units are readily available in the junk yard, or at swap meets, in outputs as high as 140 amps and sometimes more.

This alternator offers a number of advantages for a prospective street rodder looking to replace and earlier style GM alternator, or simply install a late model alternator.

The shaft size is the same as earlier alternators, which means you can install either a V-belt or serpentine pulley. The mounting lugs are very similar to earlier alternators, which makes upgrades relatively easy. And wiring is a fairly straightforward proposition.

CHARGING SYSTEM WIRING

The wires for the charging system are as

important as any wires in the vehicle. The main concern is the feed wire from the output post of the alternator to the battery. This wire must be capable of carrying the maximum output of the alternator, which may be 80 or 100 amps. Many times this wire is too small, a gauge size that won't handle the heavy current load and may become very hot or melt during full load operation. If you check the IASCA charts, a 50 amp circuit that's four feet long requires an 8 gauge wire, and 50 amps is minimal alternator output these days. In addition, use a fusible link where the alternator connects to the battery or battery power. When working near the alternator output terminal, remember that the terminal is hot all the time. A wrench laid between the terminal and the engine quickly turns into an arc welder.

Alternator exciter wires are usually small in gauge size because they are only transmitting a signal to the regulator, telling it when to charge and how much. They should, however, be at least 16 gauge to prevent too much voltage drop. Most systems require a small bulb or a resistor in the circuit between the switch and the alternator (see the diagrams in this chapter for more on alternator wiring).

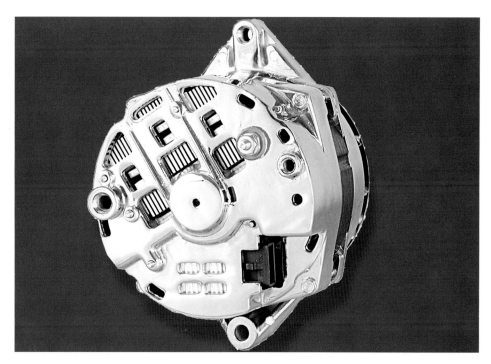

Late model units like this one have a very high output rating. Charging up to 80 amps at idle is not uncommon.

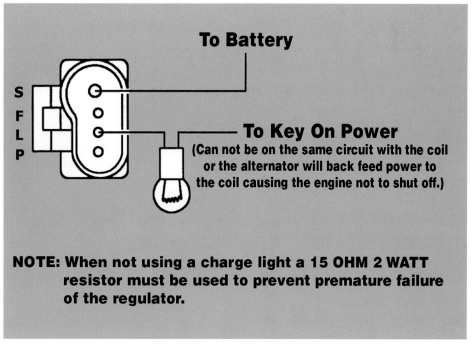

To Battery

S
F
L
P

To Key On Power
(Can not be on the same circuit with the coil or the alternator will back feed power to the coil causing the engine not to shut off.)

NOTE: When not using a charge light a 15 OHM 2 WATT resistor must be used to prevent premature failure of the regulator.

The power plug for the alternator regulator, like this one illustrated, can be easily spliced into the main charging harness

Chapter Three

Switches

Turn it On, Turn it Up

THE RIGHT SWITCH FOR THE JOB

Switches allow us to turn the power off and on in the various circuits. The topic might seem almost too simple. Yet, consider that in addition to factory switches for everything from headlights to heater fans and windshield wipers, the

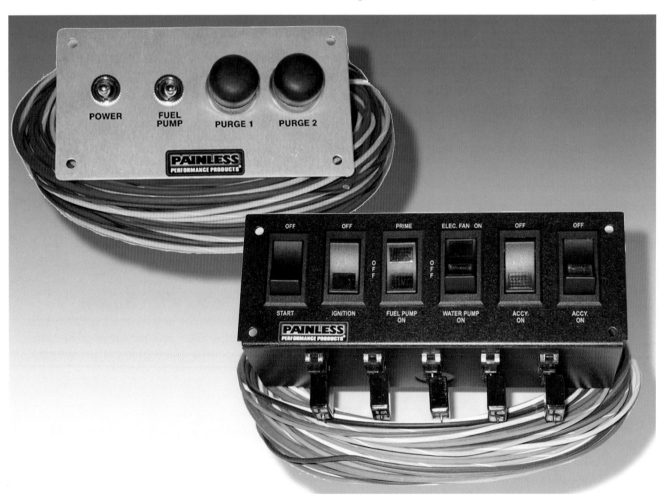

Switch panels of all kinds are used in racing, including the upper panel meant to control nitrous operation. The lower panel is designed for drag racing and has not only the switches but also the circuit protection devices and wiring harness.

aftermarket offers similar switches in "universal" styles, plus a variety of heavy duty and water-proof models.

CHOOSING THE RIGHT ONE

Switches need to be evaluated in terms of the job they have to do. Before buying a switch to serve a particular func-tion, consider the follow-ing:

1. Will the switch physi-cally fit in the desired location?

If you have a round hole in the dash, obviously you would want a round mounting stem style switch. You need to ensure that there will be enough clearance behind the dash so the terminals won't short out against a support or another component located behind the dash.

2. Does the switch have enough current carrying capacity?

Overloading the switch is probably the most common cause of switch failure. All switch-es are rated for voltage and amperage maxi-mums. In circuits where there is a large load, such as an electric fan or fuel pump, the amperage draw is greatest during start up and often over-loads the switch. By using a relay you can reduce the load on the switch and thus prevent

The upper, universal switch has one power input, with tail, park, dash and headlamp outputs. A rheo-stat is used for dash light dimming. The lower OEM-style switch is commonly used in hot rods. It has 2 inputs for safety (if you loose headlights the tail lights stay on and vise versa) as well as a dome light control.

Push button switches are often used for starter activation. The rubber boot protects against harsh environments when off roading.

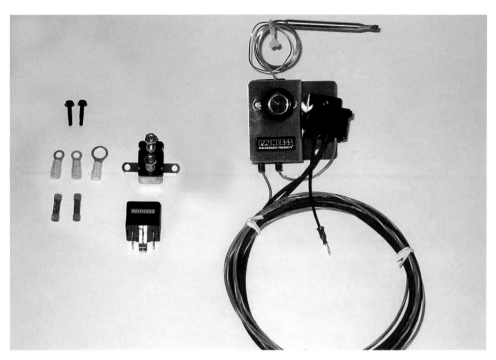

This temperature switch uses a thermocouple to sense temperature at the radiator. The knob allows the adjustment of a multitude of pre-determined settings for electric fan operation.

The dimmer switch is used in almost every vehicle to control low and high beam lights. The center terminal on the top is the input and the two side by side are the outputs. Either high or low beam wires may be attached to either terminal.

the failure. (See Chapter 5 for more on relay kits and their installation).

3. Will the switch have enough internal circuits?

A single switch may control one circuit or many circuits. The internal workings of switches determine their usage. The use of a toggle switch to operate the lighting system of a car would not be a good idea because the switch does not have enough internal circuits.

4. Will the switch have the proper hookups for the wiring?

Along with internal circuits, output terminals on the switch must match the needs of the operating device. A light switch is a good example. As mentioned earlier, a light switch has several internal circuits and will have several output terminals to transmit power. If a toggle switch were used for the same job, several wires would be required on a single terminal which presents a real problem.

TYPES OF SWITCHES

Light switches come in many different configurations. The most popular switch being used is the GM style. This switch has two internal circuits, one for headlights and one for the running lights. This separate internal circuitry allows for two battery inputs for safety. The double battery feed means that if one circuit fails the other circuit will allow the vehicle to maintain some type of lighting.

This switch has provisions for parking lights, taillights, dome lights, headlights and a dimmer control for the dash lights.

The universal style of light switch, unlike the GM style, has only one power input which may be protected by a fuse or a circuit breaker built into the switch. These switches have individual circuits for headlights, taillights, parking lights and a dash light dimmer control. Compared to a factory switch, these switches are more compact but also offer fewer features.

Toggle or push-pull switches may also be used as a light switch, though the internal circuits will be limited to one or two.

Water resistant ignition switches also play a roll in the off road market where dust, dirt and moisture can do damage.

HEADLIGHT DIMMER SWITCHES

A dimmer switch is used to direct current to one circuit or another. With a typical headlight circuit, power comes in from the headlight switch and the dimmer directs output current to the high or the low beam lights. There is no off position on a dimmer

The universal ignition switch is popular. These switches come in several configurations but usually have accessory, off, ignition-on and start positions. Most are rated for about 60 amps so caution is needed to not overload them.

A plunger brake switch (upper), can be used to control brake lights. Those with extra terminals can interface with the cruise control. A universal windshield wiper switch (lower), is common in hot rods. They usually provide for 2 speed motors as well as washer motor activation.

Rocker switches are common in all vehicles. Most, when activated, are illuminated, a plus for night time driving. Rated at about 20 amps, their uses are somewhat limited.

switch. If power is supplied the switch simply redirects it to one circuit or the other. Dimmer switches may be floor mounted or steering column mounted, though most have the same terminal configuration and perform the same function.

Some late model, column mounted, switches also provide for flashing the high beams during daylight hours as a passing signal. This provision does require a constant hot circuit (one that does not come through the headlight switch), usually the same circuit as the headlights are on from the fuse block.

IGNITION SWITCHES

As with other circuits, the ignition and starter circuits require specialized switching. The two main styles are the in-dash universal switch and the column mounted switch.

The in-dash switch is used most often when the column is designed to be straight and smooth. Vehicles built before 1969, and even some later models, had the switch in the dash or console. Some very early model vehicles used a simple off and on ignition switch, with the starter activated either by a second floor-mounted or dash-mounted push button.

As we said, overloading the switch is probably the most common cause of switch failure. The in-dash switches of today have ignition, start and accessory circuits built in. Universal ignition switches have screw terminals while factory style switches have spade connectors in a molded housing designed to accept a plug-in connector.

The only disadvantage to the modern ignition switch (especially the aftermarket style) is the amount of current it can safely handle. Some of our modern creature comforts require current draws high enough to overload the switch. The use of power relays on circuits such as air conditioning and electric fans will help prevent overloading.

Of the two styles of ignition switch, the column mount is becoming the switch of choice. With only a few exceptions, all steering columns built after 1968 had the key and ignition switch mounted on the column. On these columns the switch itself is actually mounted at the base of the column. A control rod connects the switch with the keyed cylinder. The position of these switches is adjustable in case the key position is off slightly.

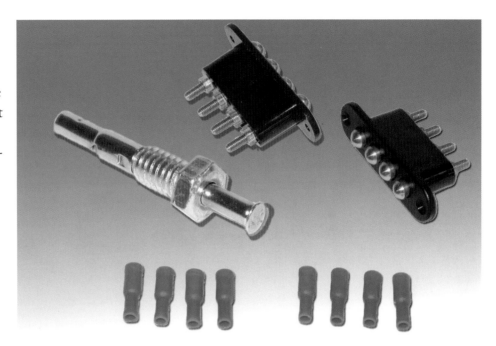

Although not a switch, these "Jambtac's" (top right) provide for current flow through the door jamb to operate power options located in the door. GM-style door jamb switches are often used to control dome light activation. These are grounding switches so the dome light would require constant power.

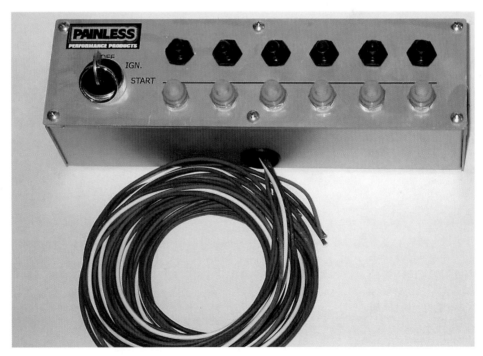

This off-road switch panel uses 2 different type switches. A water resistant keyed ignition switch, and toggle switches with water resistant covers.

Different manufacturers design the internal workings of their switches differently. The most commonly used columns and switches are the GM (Saginaw) and Ford. Both switches are equipped with multiple internal circuits and can carry large amounts of current. The main difference is in the starting circuits. GM starters use a solenoid that requires a lot of current to activate, so their ignition switch has a heavy duty starting circuit. The Ford starter,

Ignition switches are often overloaded. The switch may be able to carry lots more current than the wiring.

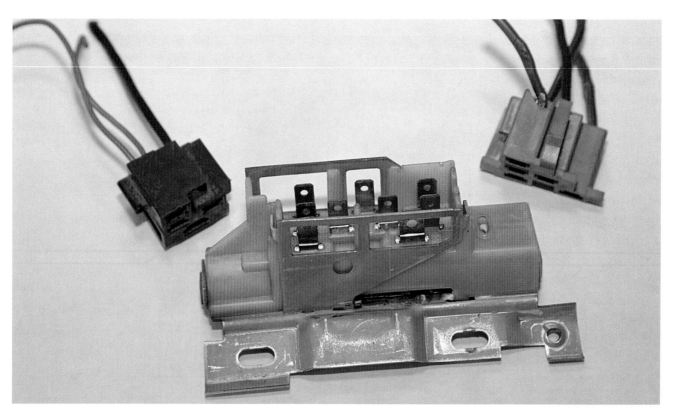

In the flesh, the very common G.M. column-mount ignition switch. Be sure to get the plugs and some wire when you buy that used column.

however, uses a solenoid that requires only a small amount of current to activate so its starting circuit is smaller and more fragile. When using a GM style starter with a Ford switch, a starter relay will be required to maintain the life of the switch.

Factory switches, whether column or dash-mounted, will generally handle more current than universal switches. Yet it is always safer to use relays for high current devices or circuits.

AFTERMARKET SWITCHES

Before buying a set of toggle switches for your project vehicle, consider the criteria discussed above. Be sure the switch is a high quality component, not a gyppo, plastic fantastic item from the who-knows-where company. When in doubt about which switch to buy and use, buy a heavy duty or aircraft switch with more than enough capacity to handle the load.

When it comes time to buy and install switches in your special vehicle, avoid the temptation to buy aesthetics over function. Remember, small and tiny switches are generally only meant for small and tiny loads.

Toggle switches come in many configurations and amperage ratings. These military spec switches are water resistant as well as rated for high vibration applications.

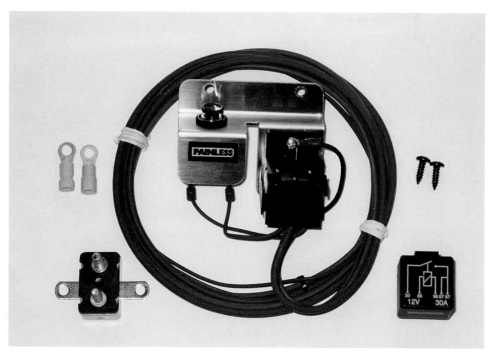

Hot starting problems are often solved with a relay such as this one that ties into the starter activation wiring. The small red switch allows the engine to be spun over from inside the engine compartment for testing and adjustments.

49

Chapter Four

Gauges

How to Choose and Install

Proper installation of your gauges involves more then just hooking up a few wires. Consider that the gauges, from the fuel gauge to the speedometer, are the most relied upon source of information in your vehicle. If the gauges are not wired properly, the information they present will not be correct.

The most common problem with gauge installations is the lack of a good ground. Since gauges are sensing devices they require only small

Dakota Digital has a large array of gauges to fit most any vehicle or need.

amounts of current (inputs) to produce their readings. With these small signals the connections are critical.

Proper grounds between the chassis, frame and the body are a must. If, when the lights or any other device are turned on the gauges read differently, the problem is a bad ground. With the large number of fiberglass parts being used today the issue of grounding becomes even more critical. A ground strap or wire may be needed between the gauges and the body or the frame. A good practice is to have a grounding lug located under the dash to help make gauge installation easier.

Outside radio frequencies, "RF noise" as it is called in the electronics industry, is another common problem. Impulse signals, such as tachometer and electric speedometer signals can be interrupted or varied by a magnetic field surrounding a group of wires. For this reason most gauge manufacturers recommend that signal wires to gauges be routed away from the rest of the main harness.

The illumination of gauges is usually simple. Most gauges today come with lights that mount directly into the rear of the gauge housing. The wire pigtail, coming out of the light, goes to the headlight switch. Some styles will have a separate wire for the ground to ensure that it is properly grounded.

Gauge clusters like these from Classic Instruments have become popular when using the original openings in the dash. Multiple gauges in a single cluster saves space and makes it easier to take in all the readings in one glance.

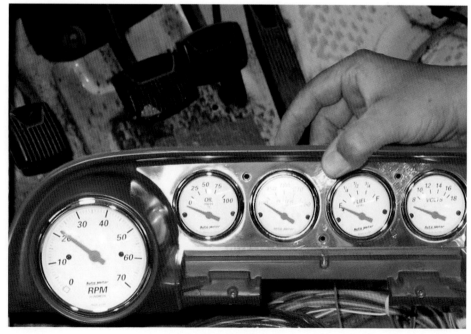

Using the original cluster with individual gauges is also attractive. An adapter in the center of this 1964 Ford dash provided for easy mounting of the 4 small gauges.

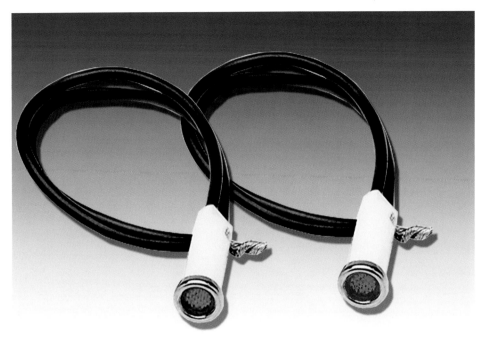

Indicator lights come in a variety of sizes and shapes. This 5/16" light is very popular because of its size and ease to see day or night.

Older-style and some commercial gauges have small windows around the outside of the gauge housing. These require that small lights be mounted in a bracket and illuminate the gauge face through the windows.

INDICATOR LIGHTS

Indicator lights for turn signals, high beam and many other circuits, are necessary to keep track of vehicle functions. These lights come in a variety of sizes and colors to fit any need. Most of these lights are wired in a common way, with one wire that runs to the proper power source and the other to ground.

Fiber optics are another type of light emitting device that is used in some applications. Fiber optics work by transmitting light through a small strand of plastic-type material. When light is focused on one end of the strand, the light flows through and is emitted out the other end. The light source is usually a light or bank of lights like normal indicators that are in a remote location. The other end of the fiber can be located wherever the light is needed. Fiber optic lights are also used to illuminate some gauges.

AMMETER OR VOLTMETER?

In the early days of hot rodding, the cool cars all ran a group of stand-alone gauges mounted in their

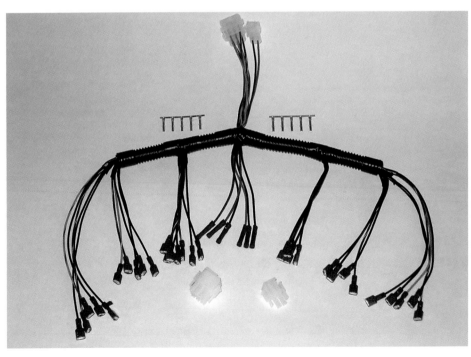

Painless Wiring makes a gauge wiring harness kit with connectors for a typical set of gauges and their lights. The wiring kits come with adapters so they will work with either slide-on terminals or round, threaded studs.

chrome plated bracket below the dash. One of those gauges was the ammeter, showing a positive or negative flow of energy, to or from, the battery.

In more recent years the ammeter has fallen from favor, replaced by a voltmeter. Men and women building a car often ask which is better, an ammeter or a voltmeter? If they don't understand, they sometimes install one and try to hook it up like the other.

First, a few definitions: An ammeter measures current flow (amps) and is installed in series. In a typical automotive application all the current needed to run the car, including all the accessories, goes through the ammeter. That means you have two large, eight or ten gauge wires up under the dash going to, and from, the ammeter. If either of these wires touches ground you have an instant arc welder under the dash. A voltmeter, on the other hand, measures the voltage in a circuit and is wired in parallel. That is, the current necessary to run the car and its accessories does not move through the voltmeter. You simply need a light wire to a source of battery voltage and another to a good ground.

There is another problem people never consider, a lot of ammeters get overloaded. Most ammeters are capable of carrying 30 or 40 amps, while the new alterna-

The voltmeter on the left measures the voltage in the electrical system. The ammeter on the right measures the amount of current flowing into, or out of, the battery. Note that the ammeter only registers up to 30 amps. This is a melt down looking for a place to happen in our later model systems.

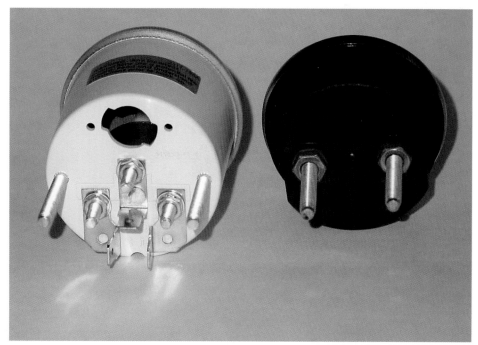

The attachment posts on the back of the gauges are also different. The volt meter on the left requires a 12 volt sensing input and a ground. The ammeter on the right has 2 posts. The main power wire from the battery source and power input to the fuse block.

Cluster assemblies, like this one from Serious Hardware, simply bolt into the factory dash. The gauges are far more accurate than the originals.

tors put out 80 to 100 amps or higher. Old ammeters can't handle the amperage, and if the ammeter overloads and quits so will the car. The old cars that ran ammeters only had a 30 amp charging circuit. The cars had no power windows and no air conditioning. But that's not the case anymore. When people ask, I always tell them to use a voltmeter.

Voltmeters are more modern, are good indicators of the charging circuitry, they're easier to hook up, and most of all they are safer in today's high current vehicles

AVOIDING TROUBLE

For some specialized information as to the best way to install a set of gauges, and avoid any electrical gremlins, we contacted the folks at Auto Meter gauges.

They report that most gauge troubles can be eliminated (hopefully before they start) by paying attention to detail as you wire the gauges. When they get a caller on the tech line complaining that the new Auto Meter tachometer is jumping all over the place, they can usually diagnose it over the phone. Jumping tachometers are usually caused by solid-core plug wires, which produce a great deal of RF noise which in turn affects the tachometer. To correctly wire the tachometer the

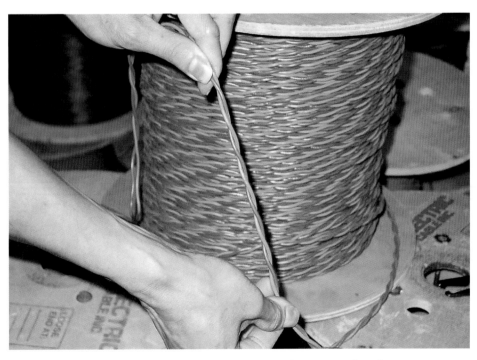

Twisted wire helps to reduce RF noise in the speedometer and tachometer circuits. These wires should still be routed away from the main harness.

green wirc should be connected to the negative side of the coil (on a standard ignition), or the Tach terminal on many electronic ignitions. Connecting to the coil terminal on an MSD ignition will damage the tachometer. When in doubt read the directions or contact the gauge manufacturer.

The other common problem with any of the gauges is caused by poor grounds. If in doubt about the quality of the ground Auto Meter recommends running a wire all the way back to the negative battery post.

Although this is a wiring book, the good people at Auto Meter recommend using anti-seize on the threads of the fitting and sender for the mechanical gauges. With anti-seize on the threads there won't be any oxidation between the sender and the block or fitting to affect the readings, and you can take the sender out in a year or two without damaging the sensitive capillary tube.

When trying to decide between mechanical and electrical gauges, remember that while mechanical gauges are slightly more accurate, electrical gauges make installation easier by using wires instead of capillary tubing. Mechanical gauges also offer a full-sweep dial face for easier viewing of precise measurements.

This gauge cluster from Dakota Digital has all the gauges in a single unit. Digital gauges are very popular and easy to install. They have their own computer and connecting cable that is easily wired into the chassis harness.

An array of dash bezels are available from numerous suppliers. Most bezels are used in the street rod industry as the later model vehicles were equipped with a full set of gauges from the factory

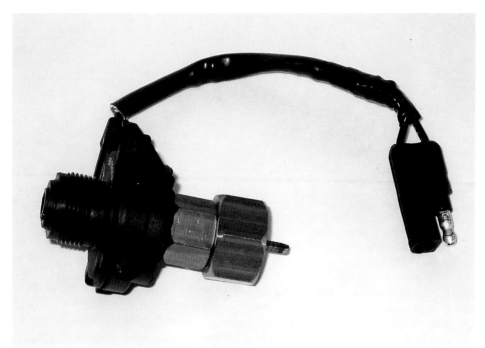

The speedometer sender shown is a common one used with cable drive outputs on transmissions. Usually the two wires coming out of the sender attach to the wires at the speedometer. Care needs to be taken to prevent these wires from getting to close to spark plug or other high current wires due to RF noise.

Another set of problems is caused by sending unit wires and capillary tubes routed too close to header pipes and other sources of heat. Neatness counts, so does common sense. The sender, for example, on a water temperature gauge must actually reach down into the water jacket to get an accurate reading. It can't be mounted away from the block in a T fitting designed to house both the gauge sender and the sender for a light.

Note: Most gauge manufacturers recommend against using sealer or Teflon tape on the threads of an electrical sending unit for fear of eliminating the circuit to ground. However, there are those real-world situations that require a little plastic tape on the threads to eliminate a leak, and in most cases the threads of the sending unit will bite through the sealer to make a good ground.

The Auto Meter technicians note that gas gauges are not all the same, and all factory sending units do not provide the same "reading" to the gauge. Most GM gauges read 0 ohms when empty and 90 ohms when the tank is full. Ford and many Chrysler products provide an almost opposite set of readings: 73 ohms when empty and 8 to 12 ohms when full. Some cars read 240 ohms when empty and 33 when full. When in doubt, use your ohm meter, connected

Temperature sending units on the later model engines, like this GM LS1, use a sealing washer instead of pipe threads. No sealing tape is required.

betwccn the sending unit connection (the one that runs to the gauge) and ground. Now take a reading with the tank empty, and full, and then refer back to the instructions that came with the gauge to determine if the sender is compatible with the gauge.

SPEEDOMETERS

With regard to speedometers, those from Auto Meter, and most others, use standardized fittings and drive cables. If the speedometer is off, correcting it might not be as simple as installing a new driven gear. To obtain correct gear fitment you may have to change both the drive and driven gears. Sometimes a correcting ratio drive joint can be used to adjust the speedometer input. These correcting ratio drives are available from a variety of specialty speedometer shops.

The new programmable electric speedometers are really nice to install. Regardless of the transmission sender, the internal circuitry will adjust during the calibration phase on the installation.

Remember to route the speedometer wires away from the rest of the main harness to prevent RF noise from giving a false reading. With any gauge, the key to accurate readings is proper installation. Take the extra time necessary for a neat installation and you will be rewarded with proper operation.

Classic Instruments offer a wide selection of gauges featuring cable driven speedometers.

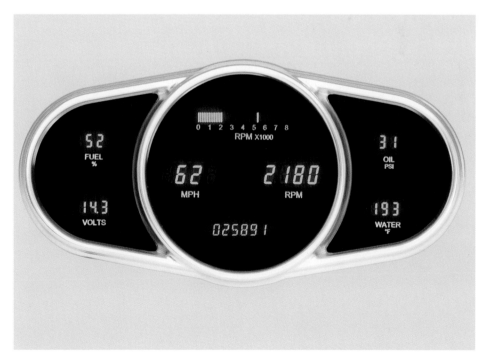

Gauges, like these from Dakota Digital, can be programmed for almost any speed sensor output.

Installing Gauges

John Roberts removes the gauges from their packaging before planning where each one will be placed in the dash.

Installing gauges is a simple project. The most nerve racking part is cutting the holes they are to be mounted in. As mentioned earlier, some clusters simply fit in the original dash openings and some fit into bezels that are pre-drilled. Such is the case with the aftermarket dash for the 1966 El Camino in this story (this El Camino is being prepared for display at the SEMA Show in Las Vegas). The dash harness used has all the wires necessary for not only the gauges but also the dash indicator lights. A set of quick disconnects are also included for easy removal for servicing if needed at a later date.

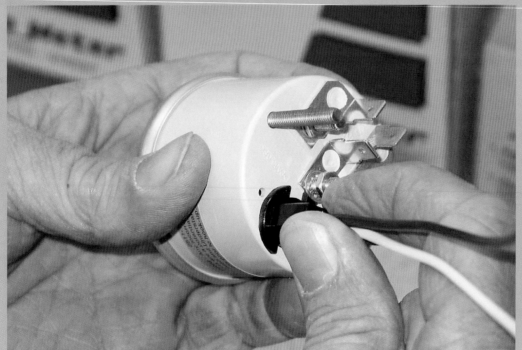

Before installing the gauges, John inserts the illumination lights into their housings. Some gauges come with colored covers for the light bulbs so they will emit a red or green hue at night. If they are to be used, they need to be installed before assembly.

The lights have been installed and the gauges themselves are mounted. Handy thumb screw nuts hold the mounting bracket in place.

John mounts the assembled cluster to the dash. Minor trimming of metal around the gauges was required for clearance.

The Painless gauge harness selected has all the wires necessary for all 6 gauges including the grounds and special wires for the electric speedometer.

The harness is spread out and checked for fit. All wires are color coded for each gauge. To insure a clean look, a couple of gauges were re-located into different holes so the wires didn't criss-cross.

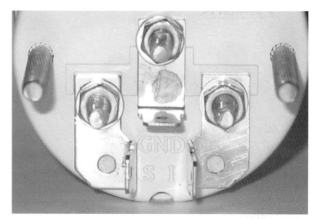

A close up shows 3 terminals: Ground (GND), the top horizontal terminal. Ign. (I), the vertical terminal on right. Sender (S) on left. With a voltmeter there is no sender so that terminal isn't used.

The Autometer gauges have male spade style terminals which makes it easy to attach the harness. Harness comes with adapter terminals for use with gauges that have threaded studs for wire attachment.

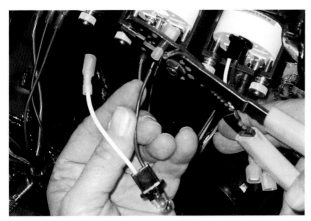

Quick connect male spade terminals are attached to the light socket leads. This will allow for the plug-in feature all across the dash.

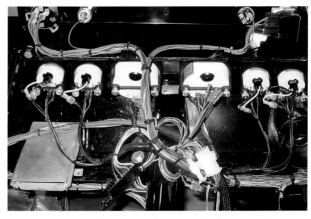

The harness side terminals were then inserted into the mating plastic housing. Care was taken to pin red to red and so on. Once finished, the harness was temporarily routed and secured.

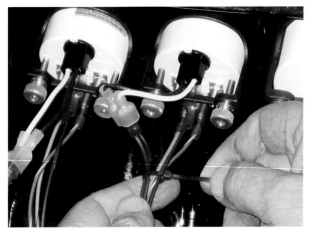

With all gauges wired, plastic tie wraps are used to loom and secure the harness. The harness can also be attached to dash braces to prevent chafing.

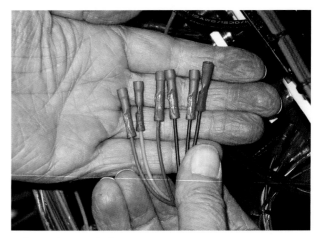

The indicator light wires were next. Wires are pre-terminated with butt splices which prevent possible shorting in the case of non-use of an indicator light.

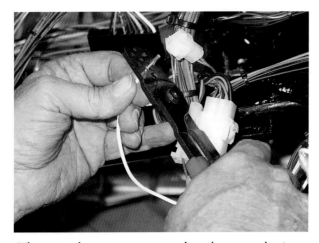

The main harness was cut to length to match pig-tail of the dash harness. Once cut, wires were stripped and the supplied terminals for the quick disconnect were attached.

John chose to remove the butt splices and replace them with push on terminals like those used on the illumination lights. This will allow the indicator lights to be changed without cutting of the harness.

With all gauges installed, it's time to attach wires to sending units. Fuel sender is installed per instructions and pink wire from the gauge is attached. Care must be taken so tank/sender is properly grounded.

The water temp. sender is next. Sender should always be placed in the engine where it is the hottest, like the intake manifold next to the thermostat or driver's side cylinder head.

Oil pressure senders come in various sizes and calibrations. Be sure yours matches the gauge. An extension pipe will help to clear engine accessories such as distributors, power steering pumps and linkages.

If a later model tranny is used (shown) the signal output may need to be shared with the engine computer. Be sure to get proper instructions, with the gauges you purchase, for your specific transmission.

This overhead view of an HEI GM distributor shows the tachometer wire output. Different engines with different style distributors will have their own requirements for hookup.

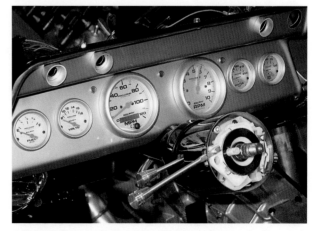

The dash installed with all the indicator lights and gauges, it makes a nice looking package as well as a functional display of what is happening in the engine compartment.

Chapter Five

Wire the Accessories

Add Circuits the Right Way

This chapter is about wiring electrical accessories, which often involves adding extra circuits. Whether you're adding circuits to an existing harness to run the power windows or looking for information on air conditioning circuits, we've tried to provide some basic wiring guidelines and in some cases, a few typical wiring diagrams. As always, there's a right and a wrong way to add circuits. You want to avoid the quick and dirty method in favor of slow(er) and sanitary.

Does your fuse block look like this? Not enough circuits? It is time for an additional accessory fuse block for those needed circuits.

ADDING CIRCUITS

Whether you're adding a set of halogen lights to your 4X4, or an electric fan to the old Chevrolet, there comes a point when you can no longer run the power through the fuse box. Even if the fuse box in question offers extra unused circuits (which many do not), there comes the issue of total current draw moving through the fuse box.

The fuse box in your car or truck can only handle so much current without suffering a melt down. When it comes time to add a circuit for the new accessory, why not just go ahead and install a second, auxiliary, fuse block.

By adding a second fuse block you isolate the new circuits and their current loads from the main fuse block. You're not asking the main fuse block to carry too much current or tagging too many new devices onto existing circuits.

When adding a second fuse block be sure it offers enough circuits to provide for current and future accessories. Decide ahead of time whether you want these circuits hot all the time or only when the ignition is on. Be sure all circuits are protected by individual fuses and that the new fuse block has enough total capacity to handle all your present and future accessory needs.

This 3 circuit, 2 ignition hot and 1 constant hot, auxiliary fuse block from Painless, allows for extra circuits to be added without compromising the capacity of the existing fuse block or wiring.

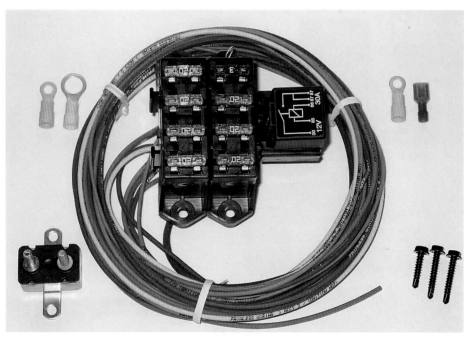

Multi-circuit auxiliary fuse blocks, like this one, will allow addition of many circuits or can be used as a primary fuse center. Like the 3 circuit, this 7 circuit unit gets its input power directly from the battery source for maximum output potential.

Auxiliary fuse blocks, like this one, are popular because one can wire it to suit the vehicle's need. They are made to snap together with one another for multiple fuse applications

Painless Wiring manufactures a series of fuse blocks that feature both constant-on and ignition-on circuits. The ignition-on circuits use a relay to turn the power on and off. An ignition-on wire is used to power the control side of the relay. When the ignition is turned on, the 30 amp relay closes, providing power for up to four circuits. A circuit breaker in the main feed circuit protects the fuse block. Each individual circuit is rated at a maximum of 20 amps.

Caution should be taken when adding accessories to your vehicle to ensure the fuse block, fuses and wiring are all heavy enough to carry the load required. Accessories such as power windows and door locks do not normally require a lot of current, but when adding a stereo and amplifier the power requirements increase drastically. In some cases the power requirements are so great that power is taken directly from the battery through a large circuit breaker or maxi fuse. Please consult the operating/owners manual for any accessory that you will be adding to ensure it is provided with an adequate power supply.

AIR CONDITIONING CIRCUITS

Adding air conditioning to an existing electrical system can easily be done,

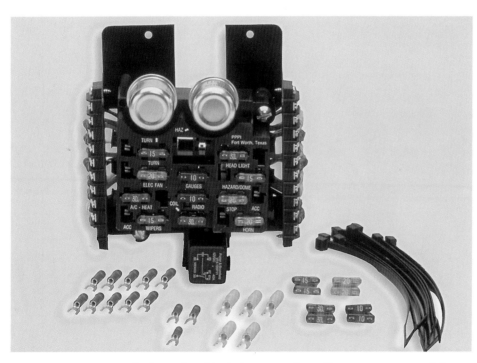

This 12 circuit, stand alone, fuse block from Painless offers pre-terminated fuse wiring as well as turn signal and hazard flashers. All the basic circuits are incorporated and it is ready for installation.

but can destroy the wiring and fuse block if not done properly.

Most air conditioning manufacturers now include a power relay harness with the A/C kit. This relay will allow the high current necessary to run the blower motor as well as the compressor clutch. The relay gets its power from the main battery source, such as the starter solenoid or maxi fuse, which does not overload the existing fuse block and wiring. As with all accessories, maximum power to the load translates to maximum output of that device (more on A/C circuits in Chapter Nine).

This diagram shows a basic cooling fan circuit. Vintage Air

Electric fans come in various sizes, buy the biggest one you can, ask if the fan has a CFM rating and whether or not it's meant for installation ahead or behind the radiator.

ELECTRIC COOLING FANS AND AIRFLOW

Electric engine and air conditioning cooling fans have become the most widely used high current consuming device in hot rods. Many of our hot rods have limited hood and radiator clearance, which reduces under-hood airflow. Electric fans are a good way to move air over the radiator and condenser, even when the car is sitting still. The fans, however, are only as good as

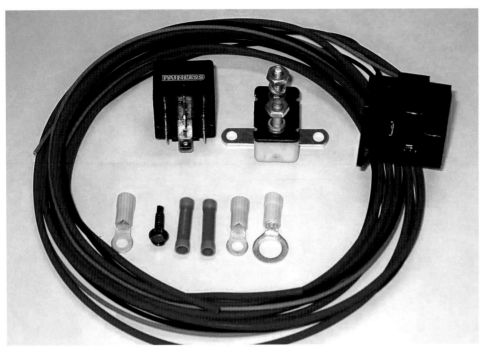

Air conditioning, with the compressor and blower fan, requires a lot of current. A universal relay can provide enough power to the system without overworking the rest of the electrical system. An older system, without a factory power relay installed, definitely should be upgraded before the electrical system fails.

their power supply. As a general rule of thumb, a fan will require 1 amp of current for each inch of diameter. During start up this figure can easily double. In other words a 16" fan will require 16 amps to run at maximum rpm and can require 32 amps to get from 0 to that maximum rpm.

To operate efficiently, a fan relay is essential, you can't just wire the fan to a toggle switch on the dash. Though many people still wire them that way, they are not getting the full potential from their fan, and they risk overheating if they don't keep their eyes glued to the temperature gauge.

An example of the loss of efficiency is often thought of in this way. If a fan is rated for maximum output at 1200 rpm with a 12 volt input, what happens if

Electric cooling fan relays have become a must in today's hot rods. Increased horsepower and air conditioning create excessive heat in the engine compartment. Fans need to be able to run at their maximum capacity and the relay will allow the maximum current to flow to the fan.

the voltage drops to 11 volts because the wiring is too small, or the circuit runs through a switch that can't handle the load? Right, the fan slows down and the cooling capacity decreases.

Mounting relays in the proper place is as important as their use. Relays are not always the prettiest and so many people mount them inside their ride under the dash. The old rule of the shortest distance between 2 points is a straight line applies here as well. The relay should be mounted between the power supply (starter solenoid or maxi fuse) and the fan in the engine compartment. Standard relays, as well as weatherproof relays, can be used depending on the application.

ELECTRIC FUEL PUMPS AND FLOW

Fuel pumps fall into the same category as electric fans. Most pumps do not require the same amount of current as a fan but the pump's efficiency still depends on the input voltage. Pumps used in racing will require much more current than on a hot rod with a small block and carburetor. As with electric fans, care should be taken to insure the circuit that feeds the pump matches or exceeds the current requirements stated by the pump manufacturer.

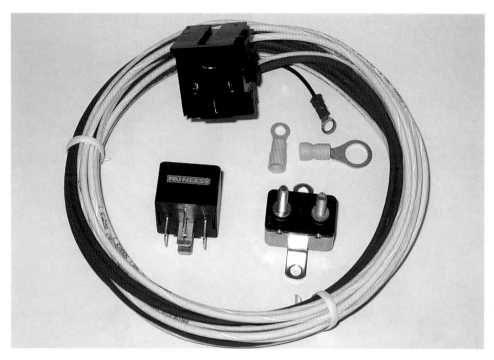

Fuel pumps don't always need a relay, but for maximum output one is always recommended. With racing pumps, a relay is a must due to the higher current requirements.

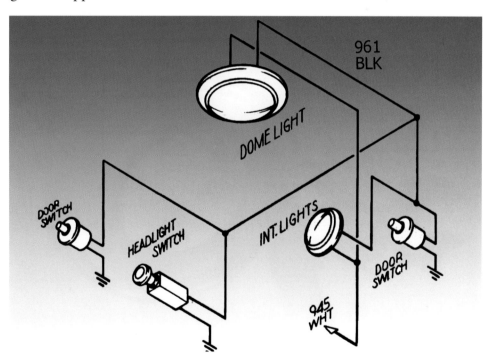

This typical dome light diagram illustrates how a grounding jamb switch system is wired.

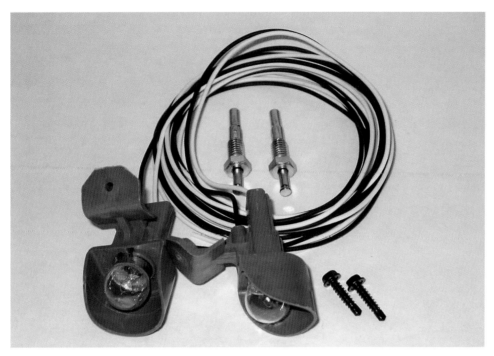

Courtesy lights are a real asset when entering your ride at night. Kits like this one from Painless make it easy to add those wanted lights for night time interior visibility.

INTERIOR LIGHTING

Interior lights are a must when trying to read a map or find something you dropped on the floor at night. Both the lights themselves and the switches are easy to install. Most jamb switches are grounding switches and only require installation into a grounded doorjamb. In fiberglass bodies a separate ground wire will be needed from the switch to a chassis ground.

If the light switch incorporates a dome light control, simply route the power wire from the fuse block to the light(s), with a ground wire to the doorjamb switch(s), or through the headlight switch. This way, if you open either door or rotate the light switch backwards, the dome light is supplied with a ground and the lights go on.

BRIGHTER HEADLIGHTS

Headlights are changing faster than most of us realize. The new halogen and projection beam lights offer much better vision at night. Installing these lights can pose a real problem though with the light switch and dimmer switch, as well as the wiring that ties it all together.

High power lights are like other power consuming items in your ride, correct operation depends

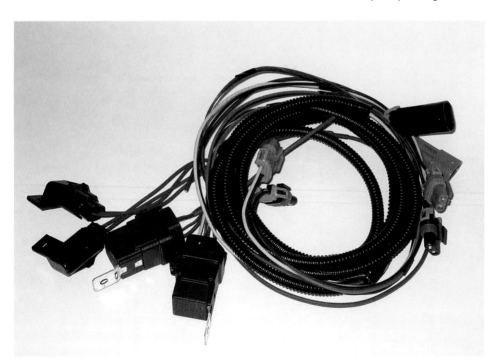

Plug-in relay kits, like this one from Painless, allow you to add the power necessary to make those new headlights as bright as possible. No alteration of the existing electrical system is required.

on a circuit that will supply more than adequate current. Power relay kits are available that are switched on and off by the stock light and dimmer switches, but the power required for the lights is provided from the battery source directly to the light through a relay. If you are one of the many who have purchased higher output lights, but find that they aren't much better than what you replaced, the electrical system may be the problem.

High beam headlight relay kits offer a simple solution to the night time vision problem. The relay allows the low beam lights to stay on when the high beam lights are turned on.

Good lighting is critical in country driving. Most GM trucks from 1987, and some cars equipped with 4 headlights, switch from the 2 low beams to the 2 high beams as the dimmer switch is activated. Instead of four lights you only activate two when the high beams are on. The solution is a relay kit that keeps the low beam lights on when the high beam lights are on. This makes a tremendous difference in visibility on those back country roads.

TRANSMISSION LOCKUP KIT

The 2004R and 700R4 Transmissions from General Motors requires electronic control of the torque converter. Most of these transmissions are factory installed in cars with computer

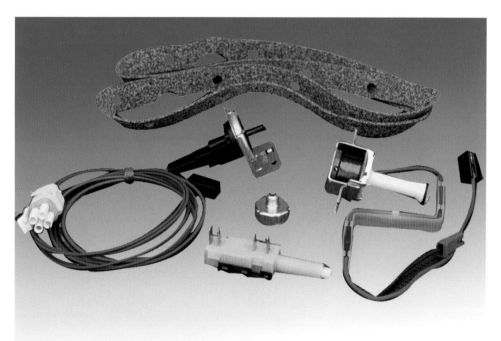

In order to properly run a 2004R or 700R4 transmission in a car or truck without a factory computer you need a conversion kit like this one so the torque converter locks up at all the right moments.

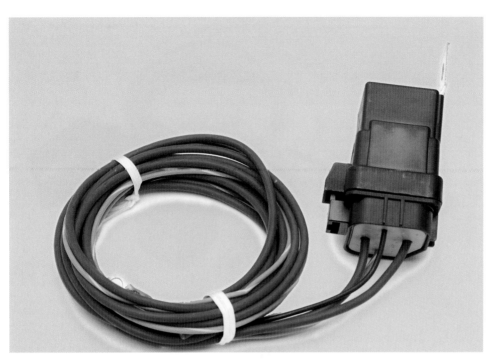

Weather-proof fan relays are also available for those extreme condition situations. An open engine compartment roadster, or a Jeep fording creek bottoms, would be good candidates for this style relay.

controlled fuel injection and ignition. That same computer provides a signal to the torque converter, telling it to lock up in 3rd or 4th gear, under light and medium load, when the car is moving. If you push the pedal to the floor or apply the brakes the torque converter reverts to non-lock-up status.

The control unit provided by Painless and some other aftermarket suppliers takes the place of the computer input for the 2004R and 700R4 transmission. The kit provides for input to the torque converter so it only locks up in 4th gear (most kits don't pro-

Need more circuits? This 18 circuit fuse center has all the common circuits as well as creature comfort circuits like power windows and locks. Just mount and add your own wires.

vide for 3rd gear lock up) under light to medium throttle with no brake application.

When you buy and install a converter lock up kit be sure there is a provision to unlock the converter when the brakes are applied (usually with a brake switch that's separate from the brake light switch). A simple toggle switch to lock and unlock the converter can be extremely dangerous in an emergency situation where there simply is not enough time to remember to turn off the lock-up switch.

As with all other electrical work, it's important to think through the addition of any circuits before you cut any wires. No matter what you add, whether it's a new killer stereo or an electric fan, you have to ensure the device is supplied from a circuit that will provide current that will match that required by the manufacturer of the stereo or fan(s). At the same time you have to avoid running too much total power through the fuse block.

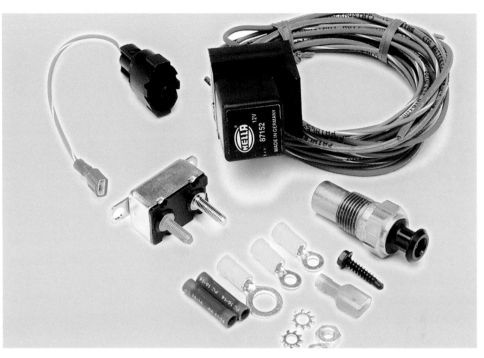

This fan relay kit has a thermostat that goes in a coolant passage and is preset to turn on the fan relay at a given temperature. These thermostats are grounding units and will burn out if attached directly to the fan ground.

200 4R transmissions are popular because of their lighter weight. Lock up kits are available for them when a computerized engine is not used.

Chapter Six

Converting from 6 to 12

More Volts, Fewer Amps

Converting from a 6 volt system to a 12 volt system is quite simple. In some cases little or no wiring modifications are required. A battery and generator/alternator change, combined with new light bulbs, covers a large percentage of the nec-essary work. Dealing with items such as the radio, gauges and heater, however, is a little more difficult and takes some cautious thought before any new components are added.

Another item from Fifth Avenue is a 6 volt alternator - if you want to give your 6 volt system a boost. It is rated at 60 amps output. Care should be taken to insure the existing wiring will be able to handle the increased output.

THE WIRING HARNESS

Wiring originally used on the 6 volt system can be reused in most cases. Since a 6 volt system requires more amperage than a 12 volt system, the 6 volt wires are usually larger than the 12 volt equivalent. An example might be a headlight that draws 90 watts. At 6 volts, 90 divided by 6 equals 15 amps, where a 12 volt light will only draw 7.5 amps (wattage divided by voltage equals amperage). The down side - even though the 6 volt wires are larger in gauge, they are also old and may need to be replaced.

DEALING WITH THE VARIOUS COMPONENTS

The ignition system will need attention. If you are changing to an electronic system then all is well. Retaining the original distributor? The points will be fine but the coil will need a ballast resistor or a coil that is designed for 12 volts without a resister.

Wiper motors are another story. A 6 volt motor may work but it won't last long and the speed may be hard to control. If you are using a vacuum unit then obviously there isn't a problem. If you decide to replace the 6 volt motor with a 12 volt replacement, then there are manufacturers, like Newport Engineering, that have motors for most stock applications.

Power window motors can usually be re-used. The speed will be faster, and as long as the switch isn't held once the motor has run the window all the way up or down it should be OK. Power top motors are like window motors. Caution should be taken not to bottom out the mechanism and strain the motor.

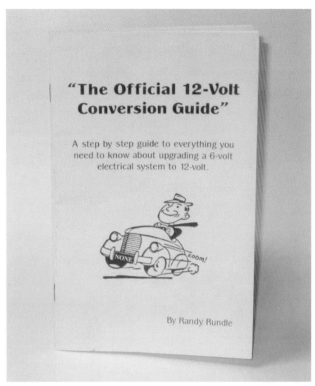

This book, from Fifth Avenue Antique Auto Parts, is a great guide to converting from 6 volts to 12. Lots of easy to understand text and illustrations make this book one to keep in your tool box.

Changing to an electronic distributor, like this HEI unit, makes the transition of the ignition system easy. The coil will need changing if the original distributor is used.

Electric wipers were a great step forward compared to the vacuum units used for years. Several suppliers make 12 volt conversion motors for upgrading.

The cigarette lighter, if so equipped, will need the element changed. Most elements can be removed from the knob to keep the nostalgia look.

Switches are another item of concern. As in the wiring, switches are usually made to handle more current than will be required by the 12 volt system. If a horn relay is used it will need replacing, or its life will be short lived. The horn may be able to be reused. Only testing will tell. Some will work fine and others go crazy and make wild sounds. Turn signal flashers will also need changing

Gauges and the radio require a specific amount of voltage for proper operation. Unlike the heater motor, these cannot use a resistor to reduce the voltage. The industry offers several styles of voltage regulators, from 1 amp up to 5 amps. A 1 amp unit, like the one from Fifth Avenue Antique Auto Parts, works well on a typical fuel gauge or other gauges that require a constant voltage. A 5 amp unit would operate most radios. Most people building a hot rod would probably change the radio to a more modern 12 volt unit during the build up. New radios require an additional wire for the memory. This wire, if using the original harness, will need to be added.

The original cigarette lighter will need to be changed or the element will burn out quickly due to the increased voltage. The element can be purchased separately, in most cases, so the original knob may be reused.

Heater motors and some power top motors can use a resistor to reduce voltage. These motors consume large amounts of current which creates heat, which in turn causes the resistance to increase, hence lowering the voltage. Care should be taken to make sure the correct number of resistors are installed. Each resistor will only carry so many amps before overheating and burning itself up. Fifth Avenue Antique also offers a voltage reducer for heater motors that doesn't get hot like ceramic reducers.

In most cases the original starter can be retained and simply operated on 12 volts. It will spin at a faster speed, but in most cases that is a good thing. The life of the windings may be cut a little short, but if the starter is not abused it will still last a long time. The starter solenoid will probably have a short life if it is not changed, however.

The battery is a no brainer. Well almost. Finding one to replace the 6 volt unit is usually easy. Some 40's and early 50's cars had odd size batteries and may take some battery tray modifications. Early Ford, and some other brands of cars, used a positive ground system instead of the 12 volt negative

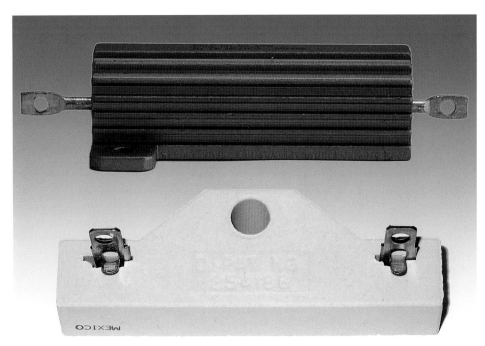

A heavy duty voltage reducer (upper) is available from Fifth Avenue Antique Auto Parts. This unit will handle more current, safer, than a standard ceramic reducer. An ignition resister (lower) is a must when converting the 6 volt points-style distributor to 12 volts. It will help reduce the arcing of the points for longer life.

The starter relay for 6 volt units operate differently in some 12 volt applications. Upgrading to a 12 volt solenoid will insure proper operation of the starter.

6 volt generators can be replaced with 12 volt units. To the untrained eye they all look basically the same. This makes it easy to retain the original look.

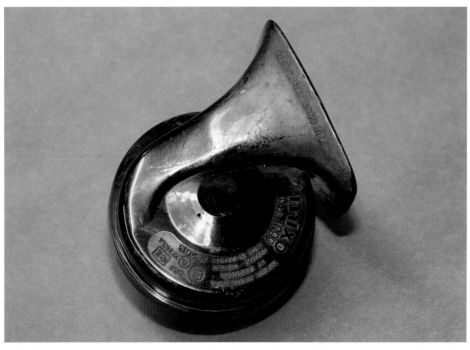

The horn may operate fine on 12 volts, but will probably sound funny. If used often, the windings will probably fail and render the horn inoperable.

ground systems of today. Since most items of concern have already been replaced with 12 volt units, the one item remaining is the starter. It should work fine on the reversed polarity. The battery cables will not need to be changed unless the ground is changed. A positive ground cable may not tighten on the negative battery post. If new cables are required, always use two gauge or heavier cable for best results.

With the battery changed, all that is left is the charging system. Converting from a 6 volt generator to a 12 volt alternator is a relatively easy task. Want to keep the nostalgia look? A 12 volt generator can be used to replace the 6 volt unit with no modification on most engines. All the late 50's cars had 12 volt generators and these are still available. The voltage regulator will need to be changed to match the 12 volt generator. Since most 6 volt wiring is larger than 12 volt wiring, little needs to be changed. An extra output wire from the alternator to the battery source, not needed when using a generator, will probably be required for safety. Brackets to mount the new alternator are readily available from many suppliers.

Converting to 12 volts probably isn't as hard as

you think. If you don't have to replace the main harness, then it's just a matter of working through the various issues and components already discussed. If the harness does have to be replaced you're looking at more work, but with the added benefits that a new harness brings to the car: things like more circuits, durable insulation, labeled wires – and of course the simple fact that the harness is, well, new.

Horn relays will need replacing to insure proper operation of the horn. Premature failure of the internal windings may occur if not upgraded.

This universal one wire unit from Powermaster was installed on the Ford spoken about earlier. The engine looks different due to some clean up and painting. All the old wiring between the generator and regulator was eliminated except for the battery wire formerly attached to the BAT terminal of the regulator, which was rerouted and attached to the output post on rear of the "one wire" alternator.

Chapter Seven

EFI for Your Hot Rod

Throw That Old Carburetor Away

Hot rods, custom trucks and muscle cars all fill one side of our garages, and in some cases, both sides. We all have our passion for a specific style vehicle that reminds us of days gone by. One of the things we have all fallen victim to is the drivability of our new daily driver. We reach in and turn the key and, without fail, the engine starts right up. Our old car, in most cases, won't do that, and instead we are pumping the accelerator and grinding away on the starter. On a cold

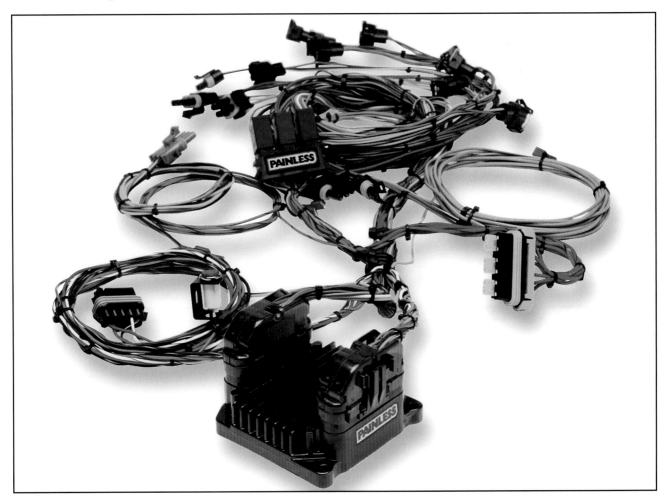

The new Perfect System from Painless Performance comes with a new Delphi computer which is pre-programmed. A truly plug and play system.

morning the hesitation, and even the dieing of the engine, gets us frustrated.

Electronic fuel injection (EFI) is becoming a way we can prevent those mornings and sometimes the name calling of our cherished ride. The biggest problem is the fear of all the electronics involved and the dependability of a system we could install. The dependability factor has been resolved by the major auto manufacturers as well as most aftermarket suppliers. Most of us never give it a second thought about driving the family car anywhere in the country, so we should be the same with our fun ride, whatever it is.

In order to help you understand these systems, decide which might be the best for your situation, and buy the right harness, this EFI chapter offers a short history, a look at current EFI systems offered by the factories, and a typical installation sequence. This chapter deals primarily with adaptation of factory EFI systems (mostly GM) to hot rod use and does not cover the stand alone high performance EFI systems available from the aftermarket.

For the street rodder or enthusiast who wants to run factory style fuel injection, this chapter should make it easier to buy the system, choose a good matching wiring harness, and install the harness.

This new corvette engine is totally different than the one Zora Duntov first designed. The electronics incorporated are far more fuel efficient than the original mechanical style.

Later model engines, even ones with super chargers like the one shown, have drivability that we have all come to expect, as well as excellent fuel economy.

Early fuel injection used high pressure pumps, valves and special nozzles to regulate fuel delivery. Daily drivability wasn't very good.

Electronic fuel injection with the old school look is becoming more popular. Fuel economy and drivability are greatly improved.

YESTERDAY'S FUEL INJECTION

One of the first post-war applications of fuel injection came in 1949 when the first fuel injected Offenhauser appeared at Indianapolis. The system was designed by Stuart Hilborn and Bill Travers, by 1953 this system was standard equipment on Offy powered cars.

The system came to be known as Hilborn fuel injection and soon crossed over into other types of racing. The Hilborn system differed from others, this was indirect (or port-type) injection, with fuel injected into the intake port just ahead of the intake valve. The port injection design meant fuel could be sprayed at a much lower pressure, eliminating the expensive and noisy high-pressure fuel pump.

At about the same time GM began researching practical applications of this new fuel injection technology. Zora Arkus Duntov teamed up with John Dolza, another GM engineer, to design a fuel injection system for the Corvette. Zora and John chose a port injection system with mostly mechanical controls. The key to any good fuel injection system is the precise measurement of the air mass entering the engine so the correct amount of fuel can be injected. The early system built by Rochester measures the air mass as it first enters the engine.

The new Rochester fuel injection system was introduced on the 1957 Corvette. Pontiac, in an attempt to keep up with the corporate Joneses, offered the same system on some Bonnevilles. Over 2,000 fuel injected Corvettes were sold during 1957. Unfortunately, the Rochester system worked better in the lab than it did in practice.

Chevrolet offered the Rochester system until 1965, but only in very limited numbers. About the time GM was eliminating fuel injection from the options list a few European manufacturers were looking into the use of fuel injection as standard equipment.

THE EVOLUTION OF MODERN FUEL INJECTION SYSTEMS

During the mid 1960's, Volkswagen asked the Robert Bosch company to design a fuel injection system capable of meeting future US emissions standards. This new system was a port, or indirect, fuel injection system. What made the system unique was the complete electronic control. Fuel was injected by solenoid type injectors mounted just upstream of the intake valves. The length of each injection pulse was determined by an early Electronic Control Module (the computer).

Rather than try to sample the amount of the air mass directly, Bosch used RPM and vacuum sensors (to determine engine speed and load) to

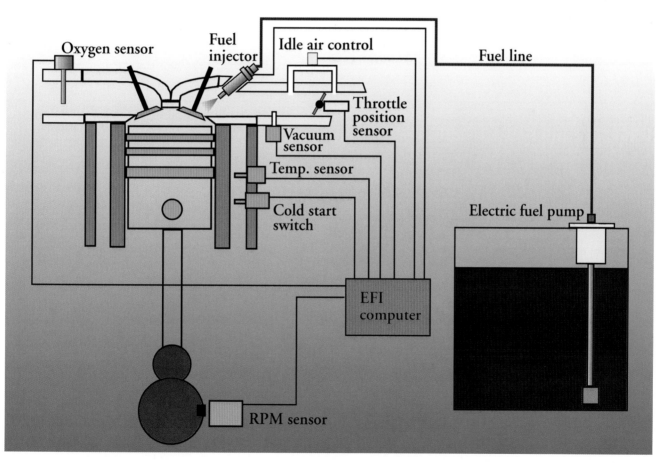

This simplified diagram shows the essentials of most electronic, port-type fuel injection systems. Shown is a speed-density system. RPM, vacuum, throttle position, temperature and exhaust sensors provide information to the computer which then decides when, and for how long, the injector should be open.

Computers come in various sizes and capacities. The one on the left is for an early TPI and the one on the right is for a late model LS1 engine. Most factory computers are also capable of controlling necessary transmission functions.

EFI Injectors come in several sizes and shapes, with different fuel delivery ratings. The 2 shown are the most common types. The injectors operate the same way, an internal solenoid, activated by the computer, opens and closes in a matter of milliseconds allowing fuel to flow into the incoming air stream.

give an approximation of total mass air. The control module used this indirect mass air measurement, modified by inputs from temperature and throttle position sensors, to determine the timing and duration of each injection pulse. More sophisticated examples of this same basic system are still used on many vehicles today. Systems that rely on this indirect means of measuring total air are known as speed-density systems.

FUEL INJECTION THEORY

The goal of any fuel delivery system is to deliver the right proportion of fuel and air to the cylinder in a combustible condition. Books tell us a ratio of 14.7 parts air to 1 part gasoline is an ideal, or "stoichiometric" ratio. The fuel delivery engineer is faced with a series of problems. First, the ideal ratio isn't always the same. Cold engines need a richer mixture, accelerating engines need a little extra fuel to maximize power. Second, for complete combustion the gasoline must atomize and mix thoroughly with the air. Third, the correct ratio must be delivered under a variety of conditions, including temperature extremes and cornering forces.

Fuel injection offers a number of advantages when compared to carburetion. Some of these advantages are inherent in the design, others are the result of modern day computer technology.

At the heart of the system are the injectors themselves. Gasoline must be mixed with air before it will burn. The mist created by the injection nozzles breaks the gasoline into very, very small particles. Smaller particles mix more readily with the air. Equally important, a very small particle is more likely to obtain enough oxygen for complete combustion. Complete combustion means more power and fewer waste products at the tailpipe.

Because this fuel mist is delivered just upstream from the intake valve, there is no problem of separation of fuel and air in the intake manifold. The throttle body can be sized for maximum performance, rather than for good air velocity in the intake tract.

Modern port injection systems tie all the injectors into a common fuel ring. Using a solenoid for an injector and controlling the solenoid with an electronic control module means great precision in delivering just exactly the correct amount of fuel. Modern systems do a very good job of measuring the air mass. That mass air measurement, coupled

This view of the Ford 4.6 engine shows the coils and the injectors side by side. Unlike most engines, the 4.6 has the spark plugs on top of the head instead of on the side near the exhaust manifolds.

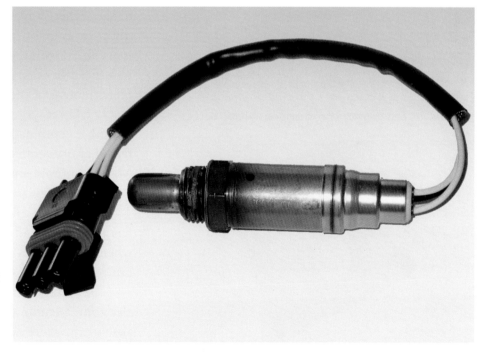

Oxygen sensors (O2) measure the amount of oxygen in the exhaust which helps to regulate fuel for maximum fuel economy. This sensor, when heated by the exhaust, will rapidly measure oxygen and send this signal to the computer for constant fuel control.

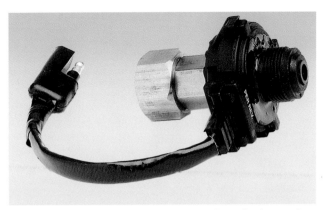

Seen earlier in the Gauges chapter, the vehicle speed sensor (VSS) is driven by the tranny's output shaft and signals the computer that the vehicle is in motion and at what speed. This information is used to help control fuel and spark for better drivability.

This weld-in oxygen sensor fitting, sometimes called a "bung," is available from Painless Performance Products. It is welded into the exhaust pipe near the engine for installation of the oxygen sensor.

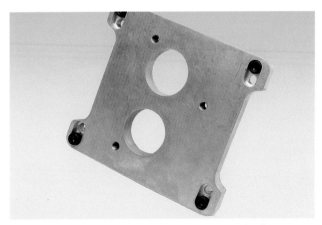

The adapter plate allows a GM throttle body EFI unit to be installed on an engine previously equipped with 4-barrel carb. without changing intake manifolds.

with information from temperature, rpm and throttle position sensors enables the control module to deliver a mixture exactly correct for a given set of engine conditions.

The precision is further fine tuned through the use of an oxygen sensor. The sensor samples the oxygen content in the exhaust and signals the control module if the mixture becomes too rich or too lean.

TODAY'S HIGH PERFORMANCE EFI

The current EFI systems used by both Ford and GM in their high performance V-8's are port type injection with electronic control. There is one fuel injector for each cylinder, mounted in the intake manifold just upstream from the intake valve. Some earlier units use a "ninth" injector to inject fuel during cold starts.

As with earlier systems, each injector is actually a solenoid. GM injectors fire once per crankshaft revolution. The electronic control module (ECM) determines the pulse width, or how long the injector will stay open. EFI systems from GM can be broken down according to how they measure the air mass entering the engine. Some of the earlier systems, from 1985 to 1989, used a direct measure of the air mass and are known as mass-air systems. Starting in 1990, GM switched to a speed-density system that relies on indirect measurement of the air mass entering the engine.

The latest systems from GM are actually a hybrid, a combined mass-air/speed-density system that uses both a MAF (mass air flow) and a MAP (manifold absolute pressure) sensor.

People often ask, which is the best system? There is no best, like anything else each system has advantages and disadvantages, especially when viewed from the unique perspective of a hot rodder.

The speed-density system uses a sophisticated electronic vacuum gauge known as a manifold absolute pressure sensor (MAP) to measure the load on the system. This MAP sensor, in combination with rpm information and inputs from temperature and throttle position sensors, provides the basic information the ECM needs to determine pulse width and timing.

With a mass-air system, the amount of air entering the engine is measured directly. The mass-air flow sensor (MAF), sometimes known as a hot wire, measures the resistance of a piece of platinum wire in the intake tract. The wire is heated by current from the ECM. Air moving past the wire tends to cool it, changing the resistance of the wire. This change in resistance is interpreted by the ECM as a change in air flow. In addition to the signal from the mass-air, these systems use inputs from the throttle position, air temperature and RPM sensors before determining the amount and timing of the injection pulse.

The ECM in either type of system is able to fine tune the amount of fuel being injected by analyzing its own exhaust sample. The oxygen sensor mounted in the exhaust system provides a signal to the ECM signaling any need for more or less fuel. This feedback or self-regulating mode used during idle and cruise situations is known as "closed loop". Open loop then describes those conditions, like wide open throttle, when the ECM operates without the input of the oxygen sensor.

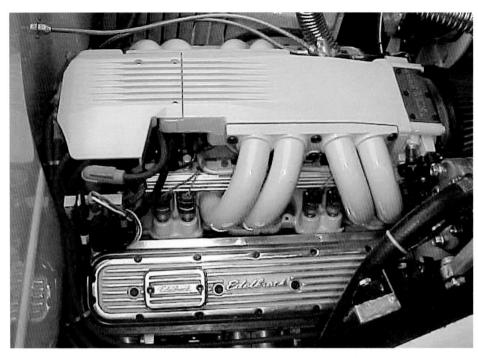

This Tuned Port Injection system is still popular today in street rods. Built from 1985 through 1992 and installed in Corvettes, Camaros and Firebirds, these engines made great torque and had very good drivability.

This MAF sensor on an LT1 engine, illustrates their position in the air intake system. They are always mounted between the air filter and the throttle body of the intake.

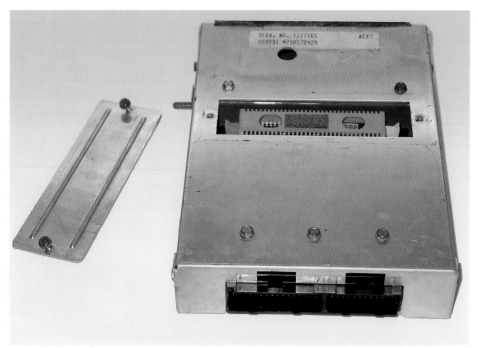

EFI has a few more tricks up its fuel injected sleeve: like control of idle speed through an idle air control, and control of the ignition timing. Because the ECM knows engine speed and load (as well as air and engine temperature, and throttle position), it is in a good position to determine the appropriate ignition timing. Through the use of a knock sensor the ECM is able to pick an ideal ignition timing figure and then roll it back slightly if that optimum figure results in a knock (another self-regulating feature).

This early GM computer has a prom, (programmable read only memory, seen in blue) sometimes known as a "chip," which may be reprogrammed for removal of VATS (vehicle anti theft system) or new fuel and spark tables for modified engines.

The major difference in the two types of EFI systems – in a real world sense – is that the speed-density EFI is designed and programmed to work with a very specific engine. These systems only know how much fuel to add during a given situation because they've been "mapped." The map provided by the factory dictates that a given set of conditions creates a particular pulse width. If you change the camshaft, or add a set of headers, the amount of air moving through that engine changes, but the map remains the same. Yes, you can change the map (contained on the "PROM" or program – more about PROMs and programs later), but it can be tough to get just the right map for your particular set of modifications.

Idle air control (IAC) motors as shown are used by the computer to control air entering the engine, which in turn regulates engine rpm at low speed. Stepping solenoids are used in many Ford applications to regulate engine RPM.

A mass-air type of system might be better suited to people who want to modify their engines, because any increase in airflow, caused by a new camshaft for example, will automatically create additional fuel (note: in this scenario you may still have to get a new aftermarket chip that will provide optimum timing for the new modified engine).

At this point it might be instructive to describe the ECM, computer, or black box that drives these modern fuel injection systems.

The computer truly is a black box, black in the sense that it is sealed from any tinkering on our part. The only part you can readily change is the PROM, which is used in 1992 and earlier engines . Re-programming or flashing is what's required in all later model computers. The PROM/program contains the specific timing and fuel injection instructions for each specific model of car. By installing an aftermarket PROM (sometimes known as a chip) or re-flashing, you are able to change the amount and timing of the injection pulse under certain conditions as well as the ignition timing and curve. The PROM/program also contains the VATS information (Vehicle Anti-Theft), meaning that unless you use the key and lock cylinder that came out of the new car you will again need an aftermarket PROM, re-program or a VATS module. A VATS module is a device that sends a signal to the computer making it think the proper key is in the ignition. Different modules are required for different year model computers.

Also contained in the computer is the Cal Pak or calibration package. The Cal Pak contains the

instruction for the "limp home" mode. Limp home is one of the computer's three basic operating modes (the other two being open-loop and closed-loop). Limp home is the mode the computer operates in when it senses a major malfunction. In this mode, the computer uses a very limited fuel curve and limits ignition timing to a total of twenty-two degrees. It's function is to not leave you stranded and allow the vehicle to be driven for repairs.

WHAT'S OUT THERE –
Current GM and Ford systems - How to Tell Them Apart

The six most common EFI systems currently being used on hot rods are:

1). Throttle Body fuel injection (TBI), used on cars and trucks from about 1987 to 1995. These were used on 4.3, 5.0, 5.7and 7.4 engines.

2). The Tuned Port fuel injection system (TPI), used on both 305 and 350 cubic inch engines. This system came in early and late versions. The early version, from 1985 to 1989,

Manifold atmospheric pressure sensors (MAP) (GM/Mopar) and barometric pressure sensors (BPS) (Ford) are used in EFI engines to inform the computer of the pressure inside the intake manifold, this information helps the computer to regulate the amount of fuel required for operation.

Illustrated is a typical 5.0 Ford computer. This computer operates the EFI system, but has no transmission functions. Early Ford overdrive transmissions did not require electronic control but had mechanical and hydraulic internal controls.

Mass air flow sensors (MAF) like the one shown measure the amount of air flow entering the engine and provides this information to the computer.

used a computer with two electrical plugs, a ninth injector for cold starts and a MAF sensor to directly measure the volume of incoming air. The later 1990 to 1992 TPI systems use a computer with three electrical plugs, no ninth injector, and a MAP sensor instead of a MAF sensor. These are speed-density systems.

3). The LT-1 system, used from 1992 through 1993, which looks totally different than a TPI system, uses its own computer, no conventional distributor and an oxygen sensor in both sides of the exhaust. The LT-1 uses a MAP sensor and is a speed-density system. The newest system from GM, the LT-1/LT-4 used from 1994 to 1996 is a combined mass-air/speed-density system with both MAF and MAP sensors. LT1 engines were either a 4.3 V8 or a 5.7 V8.

4). The LS1 system is used on the 1997 5.7 and newer generation engines in GM cars. This system has no distributor and individual coils for each cylinder mounted on both valve covers. The computer receives signals from the crank sensor, mass air flow sensor, throttle position sensor, oxygen sensor and camshaft sensor to determine spark and fuel delivery.

5). The Vortec system is used on GM trucks from 1996 to date. The 1996 to 1999 had a central injector plug and the 8 injectors were under the manifold.

This system, and all Vortec systems, are MAF. In the later 1999 and newer engines, they are like the LS1 engines with the coils mounted on the valve covers.

6). The most popular Ford engine is the 5.0 used from 1987 through 1995. These were either MAF of MAP engines depending on the original vehicle. The MAF engines, mostly used in Mustangs, are the most abundant. These engines are port injected and still use a distributor to send a signal to the ECM. These engines also use O2 sensors in each exhaust pipe.

"The easiest way to distinguish the system you have," explains Brian Montgomery from Painless Wiring, "is by checking the computer that came with the engine. The early one has two plugs (early tuned port 1986-89) and the later TPI system has three plugs (1990-92)."

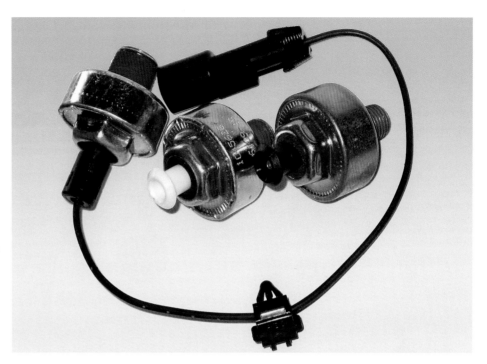

Knock sensors are used to detect detonation or pre-ignition. The computer uses this information to determine if it needs to retard ignition timing.

BEFORE YOU BRING ONE HOME

EFI engines are common at the junk yard or swap meets these days. Bringing one home is easy, and a variety of wiring and installation kits make the conversation to hot rod use very straightforward. In spite of all these aids there are a few mistakes people make on a regular basis. Mistakes that can make the job of installing a fuel

The new LS2 GM engine also has a coil per cylinder. GM uses a short plug wire rather than the coil mounted directly on the plug. The computer controls the timing of each coil's output spark for maximum performance and fuel economy.

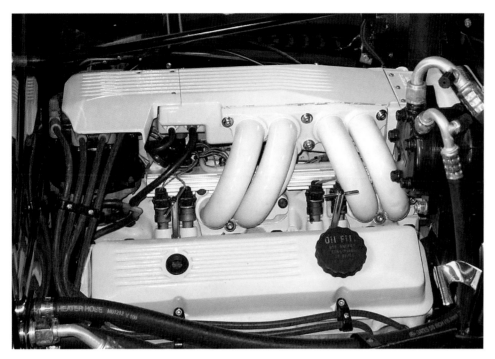

Tuned Port engines are readily available from donor vehicles. Great drivability and low end torque make them a popular choice.

V6 engines are popular in hot rods with a small engine compartment. Horse power ratings for V6 engines are close to the V8's.

injected engine in your car or truck much tougher and more expensive than it needs to be.

The first thing one needs to do when buying an engine is to be sure the engine you buy is really complete. "The buyer needs to get as many parts as possible when they buy the engine, to make sure it really is complete. That way you save the time and trouble of chasing parts, and the expense of buying them. Most important, you know that the parts on the engine are the right ones. People get an engine that's missing some parts and they try to mix and match relays and sensors and it really screws everything up. When they call here we explain that they must follow the parts list that comes with our instructions, to the letter. But the easiest way is to just buy an engine that comes with the computer, the distributor (for non-LT-1/LS1 engines) and all the right sensors and relays" says Brian Montgomery, Engineering Manager at Painless.

Another common topic on the Painless Tech Line is the relative advantage of the mass-air or speed-density systems. To quote Brian again, "I think the mass-air system, as used on the early TPI units, is better because you can make more modifications to the engine and the system will automatically compensate. With mass-air it's measuring the amount of air. With speed-density, if you make very many changes you need to have a custom chip burned from a company like Fuel Injection Specialties and some others. A speed-density system can self regulate to some extent but it's limited. I tell people with a speed-density engine that it's better to leave the engine stock."

"You need to know how you want to run the engine (mass-air or speed-density) before you buy an engine. That way you will get the correct equipment right away, including the right computer. It can be tough to convert from one system to the other, it's easier to just get what you want right away."

"There are a few quirks too. Like the 1985 TPI engine. These are all by themselves, the computer and everything else is different. But the engine is the same, so you can use the 1986 and later harness, computer and fuel injection parts on a 1985 engine."

Testing of the Perfect Fuel Management system was taken to the track. The two 1938 Chevrolets made several passes down the drag strip to verify performance gains and wide open throttle response.

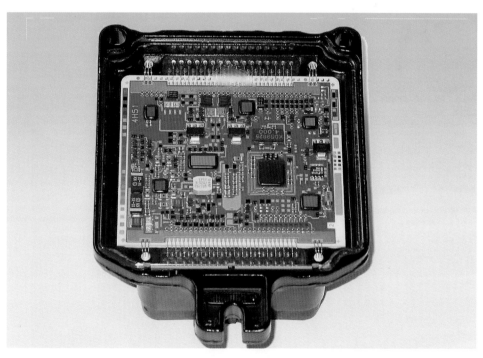

This internal view of the Painless Perfect computer made by Delphi shows the complex circuitry that provides for many, many decisions per second. This computer doesn't have transmission control functions built in.

Install Sequence, EFI Conversion on '34 Ford

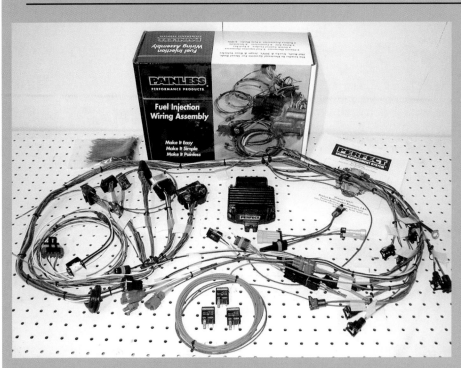

The Perfect kit comes with the new harness and nearly all wire ends pre-terminated. The new computer, a Delphi unit with programming by Painless, is a simple 2 plug installation. All needed relays, wire ties and instructions are also included.

The fuel pump is a Mallory unit regulated to 50psi. Most any style of on-frame or in-tank pump will work as long as the pressure and flow rating is adequate. Good filters are also a must.

To ease the fear of adding EFI to your car, Painless Performance has just come out with their new Perfect Engine Management System which allows you to install an EFI engine or convert your existing engine to EFI. The system has a new, pre-programmed computer, and a wiring harness that just plugs in. No laptop is required or expensive shop labor time. With only the ignition wire, fuel pump wire and the optional electric fan and a/c compressor wires to terminate, it is a no-brainer. These systems are for stock engines, but later on down the road if you decide to make some performance changes the computer can be re-programmed.

To illustrate just how simple a conversion really is, Lance Packard at Painless is going to install an LT1 system on a 1934 Ford, 3 window coupe. The installation time of the computer and harness was about 3 hours. Before Lance started, the engine, fuel system with return lines, and the chassis harness were already installed. So when Lance finished he could start the engine. Once finished, Lance turned on the ignition, the check engine light came on, the fuel pump came on and primed the system. When he turned the key to start the engine fired in about 4 revolutions. A truly Painless way to add EFI.

The following photos and text will give you information on how to install a typical EFI system on any vehicle.

The stainless tank has the outlet and return in the same basic location. Some tanks have the in and out fittings on the top. The key is to have no restriction in the system.

The wires are routed from the interior out because of the size of the connectors. The engine compartment will be wired first so any excess wire can be pulled back inside and hidden.

When Wade purchased his headers the oxygen sensor fitting was pre-installed. The new sensor mounted easily. Don't forget to add anti-seize to the threads for removal of the sensor at a later date.

All of the wires in the engine compartment except the A/C compressor wire are pre-terminated. Each group has a tag showing its destination. Both of these plug into the coil.

The prep work now finished, Lance mounts the computer up under the dash.

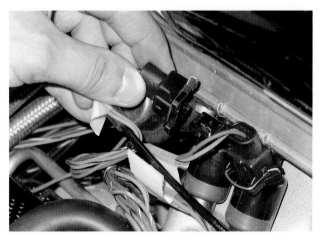

The injectors are next and all are numbered.

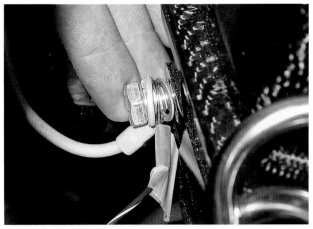

Both ground wires have ring terminals attached. There is a ground wire for the left and right heads.

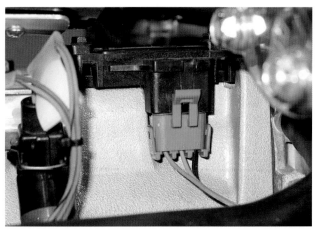

While in the same area, the manifold absolute pressure (MAP) sensor was also connected.

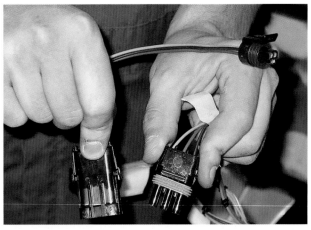

LT1 engines have been equipped with either a flat or round 3 wire throttle position (TPS) sensor. Adapter is included in the Perfect kit for either application.

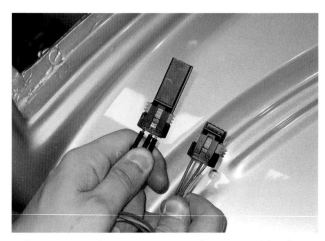

The Opti Spark ignition system has 2 possible plugs. The early LT1 engines use the short plug and the later use the longer. The Painless kit comes with both.

With the adapter installed, it simply plugs in, as well as the idle air control (IAC) connector.

The Opti Spark connector is hidden behind the water pump on the passenger side top.

The last wire on passenger side is the A/C input wire. This wire, when attached to the compressor power wire, raises the engine RPM when the compressor comes on.

The wires are now neatly arranged on the engine and the excess is pulled back into the interior. A grommet is installed for wire protection.

The 2 coil plugs are installed as well as the ignition control module. The intake air temperature (IAT) sensor was also hooked up. It was mounted in the air cleaner out of sight.

The relay bases are attached under the dash. Once attached, the relays will be plugged in.

The last wire on the engine is the main power wire that attaches to the battery post of the starter. Yes, the battery is disconnected.

The 2 computer connectors are installed. They are different and will only go in their designated port.

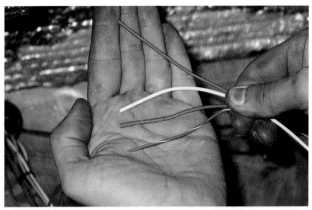

The wires inside to be terminated: 2 pink wires go to ignition source, a white tach signal wire, and a green/white relay ground for the radiator cooling fan. Computer will turn the fan on at 200° off at 185°.

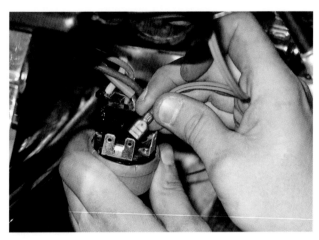

The 2 pink wires were terminated together and attached to the ignition switch. The switch terminal must be hot in start and run positions.

Lance re-attaches battery cable and turns on the key. Check engine light comes on and fuel pump primes system. A quick check for fuel leaks and with the turn of the key to start, the engine comes to life.

FINAL THOUGHTS ON WIRING YOUR HOT ROD

• Wiring a hot rod can be very intimidating to some and boring to others. The key to any wiring installation is patience. Routing of the wires is easy but routing them neatly, away from hot spots and hinge points, can sometimes be a challenge.

• Before starting any wiring job, take the time to read the installation instructions that came with the product. Little details can be the key to a successful installation and the manufacturer will usually try to inform you of these.

• Proper tools are also a must. Good quality crimping tools, a test light and a volt-ohm meter will make the job easier. Don't forget the regular hand tools for removing the seat or panels to gain access to those hard to get to areas.

• Testing of a system is also a key element of an installation. Use a small battery charger with an internal circuit breaker of 10 amps or less, to check all circuits before attaching the battery cables. If there is a problem in the system, the internal circuit breaker will trip before damage is done to wiring or connections.

• Safety is always a major concern. Always take off any jewelry or anything else that can create a short. Burns are very painful and can happen in an instant.

• Wiring is not a glamorous task. Everyone agrees that bolting on a new shinny set of wheels or some chrome goodies is fun, but if the wiring isn't done properly all that new bolt-on glitter won't do much good.

I hope you have enjoyed the information I have provided for you as much as I have had putting it on paper. We all learn something new each day and I know there will be changes in electrical systems from now on.

A quick ride down the street is in celebration of the completed installation. With the engine segment of the project done, Wade can now finish the rest of the car

Developing the Perfect Engine Management system and programing the computer meant hours and hours of run time on the dyno, followed by plenty of road testing in the real world.

Install Sequence

'64 Ford

With gasoline prices going through the roof, everyone is looking for a way to get better fuel mileage and still have enough power to get that classic out on the freeway. When you compare the drivability of a new fuel injected car, with an old, "pump the accelerator a few times, pull the choke and hope it starts," car, the easy starts and awesome drivability of the EFI car always comes out on top.

Lance Overholser was in exactly that situation with his 1964 Ford Custom 300. The car came from the factory with a 289 engine, two-barrel carburetor and a three-speed transmission. On a typical day it would get around 15 miles per gallon. Not really all that bad for a full size car, but not great. Lance wanted better mileage and better drivability.

As Lance thought this over, he asked himself, "why can't I put an EFI unit off a Ford 5.0 V-8 onto the 289?" The hunt was on for the hardware. Soon an EFI unit was found off a 1987 Mustang which seemed to be in real nice shape. Lance then visited his local Ford Racing dealer, ordered a computer kit, which included a mass air flow sensor (MAF), and a relay kit which included the oxygen sensors and barometric pressure sensor. The last major item Lance needed was a wiring harness so he contacted Painless Performance and obtained their 5.0 harness (part number 60510) which is designed for the 1987 through 1993 Ford engines.

With all the basic parts in hand, it's time to start the process of putting it all together. Lance contacted the tech guys at Painless and for a little help and some hands-on experience. The boys volunteered to come help on the project since it was being done in the Ft. Worth area.

Most of the story can be told in the photos and captions that follow, there are just a few more issues that require more explanation than can be provided in the captions:

1. Providing for an Oxygen sensor proved difficult, yet we had to put Oxygen sensors in the exhaust pipes. The decision was to use the later model 5.0 manifolds (note the nearby photos) with the O2 sensor holes already machined in since, this worked well since the exhaust system needed replacing anyway. The problem was that the clutch linkage was right in the way of the

The completed installation with fabed hose for air intake and MAF sensor, and a small K&N filter. Plenum top cover plate reads backward as noted in the text.

downward turn of the manifold. An old trick came into play, we cut a section from the cross shaft and moved it out with some flat stock. With proper bracing it allows the cross shaft to pivot around the manifold flange. It worked great.

2. Mounting the barometric pressure sensor and relays. The harness fuse block, barometric pressure sensor and relays were mounted to the kick panel (note the photos). The red diagnostic connector at the top and the black timing connector will need to be accessible when the engine is first started for any needed adjustments.

The under hood of the '64 is all original and it shows that the little old lady who bought it new didn't do much cleaning on the engine.

3. Scanning. Brian Montgomery, an engineer at Painless, checked the system after starting with the scanner, and made adjustments to the timing and throttle position sensors. When this is finished Lance can make the first test run.

4. The finished installation (check the nearby photos). Note, the hosing was fabricated for the air intake and mass air flow sensor, and a small K&N filter was installed. Notice also the plenum top cover plate reads backward due to the installation of the upper unit's air intake on the driver's side. Mustangs pull air from the passenger side but due to clearance problems with the air filter, it was decided to put the air intake on the driver's side.

Before assembly the 5.0 parts were sand blasted and painted Ford Perf. Red. Shown are the manifolds, fuel pump, computer, wiring, distributor, MAF sensor, fuel lines and the small parts.

The fender wells and firewall were re-painted so now was the time to disassemble the engine. Jeff Abbott, an engineer at Painless, removed the intake and exhaust manifolds from the 289.

James Fox, one of the Painless tech guys, installs the lower half of the intake on the engine. 289 intake gaskets were used because the 5.0 gaskets wouldn't totally seal the water ports.

The fuel rails were cleaned and installed along with the injectors.

Dale Armstrong from Painless assembles the distributor which comes with a cast or billet gear. When installing the TFI module on the distributor, don't forget the special heat transfer grease.

The assembled distributor was dropped into place. The oil pump drive is longer on the new style distributor but installed with no problem.

The decision was made to mount the computer on the passenger side kick panel. A hole was then cut under the heater for the engine compartment wires to pass through.

Routing of the wires and connectors is made easy because Painless tags each one, i.e. this one goes to the mass air flow sensor. All wires in the harness are also color coded using the original Ford colors.

We routed the air intake on the car's left side. MAF sensor is located between the K&N filter and the intake plenum (note opening photo on page 98).

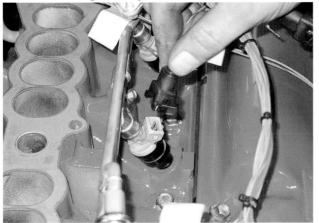

While installing the injector plugs we found a problem. The harness is designed for the 5.0 which has a different firing order than a 289. Injector plugs had to be moved to their respective firing order positions.

With the new Ford coil mounted, the harness can be plugged into both the coil and the distributor.

A couple of injector wires had to be lengthened. Wires were cut and spliced, then covered with heat shrink for their protection. The other wires were long enough and were easily re-routed.

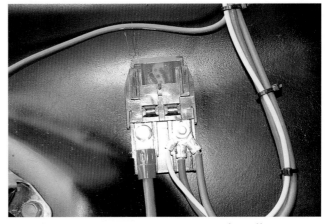

One last engine compartment wire is the yellow main battery feed wire for the computer, attached to the Maxi fuse along with other wires going to the chassis harness fuse block.

The engine wiring is completed. Fuel lines are next.

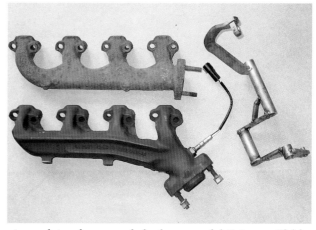

As explained, we used the later model 5.0 manifolds (lower one in the photo) with the O2 sensor holes already in place. The modified clutch cross-shaft cleared the exhaust.

Electric fuel pump was purchased from Arizona TPI and installed on the rear of the fuel tank. Special high pressure hose was used between pump and the new steel lines. The wire for the pump from the fuel pump relay was routed and attached.

With the engine side of the firewall wiring completed it's now time to mount the computer with the fabricated aluminum straps as shown.

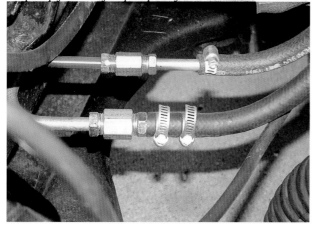

The lines installed were 3/8" pressure and 5/16" return. The return was routed to a fitting installed in the original tank drain plug.

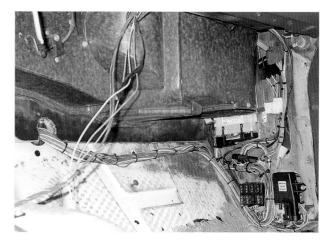

Harness fuse block, bar. pres. sensor & relays mount to kick panel. Diagnostic conn. at the top and the black timing connector need to be accessible. Wires hanging in foreground attach to fuse block.

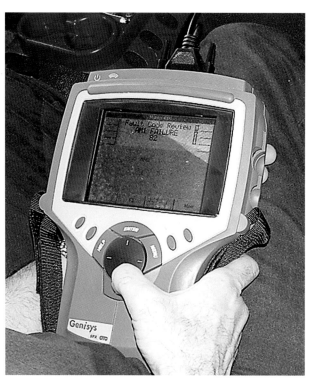

With everything installed, the ignition was turned on and the fuel pressure came up and stabilized once the lines were filled.

Here's Brian and his scanner checking the system, the timing, and the throttle position sensors.

Lance preparing the '64 for a road trip. A few days later Lance drove the car back to Indiana where he lives and called to report the car got 20 miles to the gallon. Not bad for a car with a 3.73 rear gear doing 3000 rpm at 70 mph.

Chapter Eight

Complete Harness Install

With Two, Start-to-Finish Projects

WHAT KIND OF HARNESS DO I NEED

Wiring harness kits come in many different configurations. Everything from universal, to vehicle specific, from color coded to all one color, with writing on the wires and without

writing, dash area only or engine compartment only, the list goes on and on. Choosing the right one for your vehicle is important for proper fit and the number of circuits required. The three questions you need to ask to determine

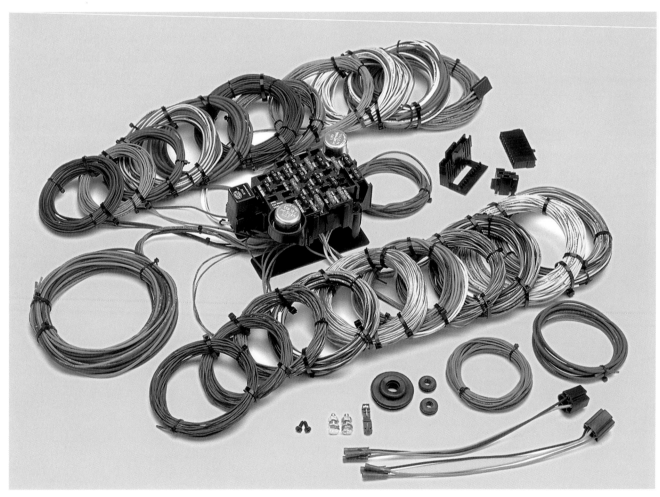

Harnesses come in many configurations. This one, called a trunk mount, has extra length as well as heavier gauge wires so it can be mounted anywhere in the vehicle. This style harness comes in various numbers of circuits depending on one's requirements.

the right harness kit are: what is the vehicle, how many circuits are required and where is the fuse block to be mounted? With these answers, a good harness selection can be made.

GETTING IT WIRED

In this chapter we install two harnesses, one in a 1937 Plymouth and one in a 1964 Ford Custom 300. Though each installation is going to be unique, the two shown here will give you a general idea on how to proceed and some of the dos and don'ts. Installing a harness is a time consuming task. Repetition is common, running a wire and terminating, again and again. Like most tasks, patience is a must to insure the job is done right. When finished, wiring is one thing you may never see in a vehicle, but also one of the most important in terms of dependability.

The Plymouth uses a typical universal harness that's designed to fit nearly any vehicle, because no two street rods are the same. Wires for the engine compartment pass through the fire wall using a rubber grommet. the fuse block is mounted using a bracket or holder. The Ford uses a different style universal harness because it's a later-model vehicle. In the later cars, such as the 1964, most have a bulkhead connector for the engine har-

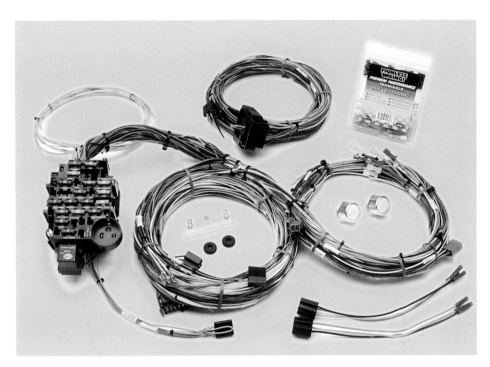

Another example of a universal harness is this 18 circuit model from Painless. The fuse block has 18 fuses, but there are 21 different circuits total. Some circuits, such as back up lights and cruise control, share a common fuse.

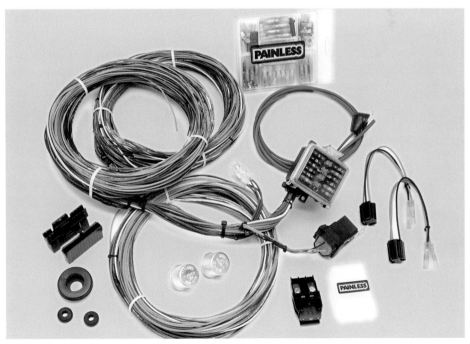

Water resistant harnesses are also available. This one has a water tight cover on the fuse block and all the terminals are heat shrink crimp style to make a weather resistant seal. Don't be afraid to ask which harness best fits your needs.

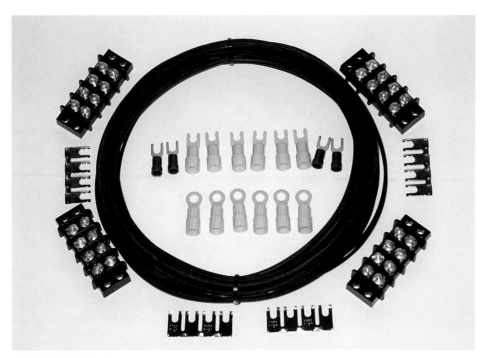

ness. Most of these were two-piece, requiring two holes in the firewall, until about 1967 when a one piece was used. The one piece was actually two or more parts locked together to make one square unit. The fuse block is mounted directly to the fire wall and the engine side connector bolts to it.

For the most part, harness kits are pre-engineered with the correct size wire for each circuit. Care should always be taken in your planning stages, however, to insure there are no circuits that may require more current than is engineered in by the manufacturer. An example might be a radio circuit. Typically a radio

Doing a fiberglass car? A ground wire kit like this one can solve a multitude of problems. The terminal strips provide a place to route those light, instruments and switch ground wires. A single large wire then connects to the frame or other chassis grounding point.

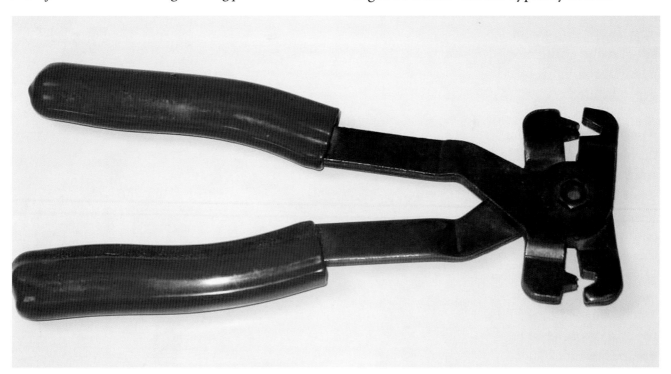

Tools are needed in wiring as in anything we do to a hot rod. This tool, off a local tool truck, is designed to crimp non-insulated terminals like used in fuse blocks and quick disconnects.

requires less that 5 amps, but if the amplifier is in the radio it may require 20 amps. If this is the case an additional circuit may be required. Most product manufacturers will have the current requirement on their instruction sheet.

The wires in a harness have several enemies.

Heat from an exhaust pipe can melt the insulation or even catch it on fire. Route wires away from hot areas as much as possible. Chaffing or scuffing is another problem. If a wire is too close to a hood hinge and is constantly rubbing there, the insulation won't last long and a short is in the making. Be sure to always route the wires away from moving parts

This closer look at the non-insulated crimp tool reveals that when squeezed the terminal is rolled around the wire into a double hump design. This style crimp works best on terminals that will be inserted into a plastic housing.

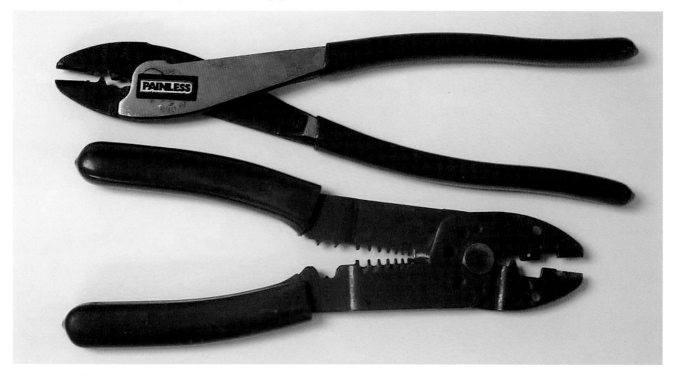

These 2 tools are most commonly found in tool boxes. The blue handle one has a variety of features such as machine screw cutting, wire stripping as well as crimping. The black/red handle tool crimps and cuts only.

Most terminals, when made, have a split in the barrel where the crimp will be. This split should always be opposite of the dimple die of the crimp tool as shown. Crimping with the dimple in the split will not make a strong connection.

so they can't be pinched or cut.

Corrosion can be the death of a connection. In some areas of the country where salt is spread on the highways, and others where salt is in the air from the ocean, corrosion can be a huge problem. When routing wires along the frame or in fender wells, be sure to protect them with a covering like tape or loom material. Be sure to support them solidly so the weight of mud or snow will not pull them apart.

Machine crimps of terminals and splices are exact each time. Care is taken to insure the crimp has the correct tension on the wire for maximum current flow.

SOLDER OR CRIMP

There is always discussion on the pros and cons of soldering or crimping connections.

As a general rule, crimping of connections is used for most typical automotive applications. Crimped terminals are easy to use and are covered with insulation which also serves as a flex restraint. A good crimp tool is required of course. Poor crimps can cause wires to come apart, or in some cases not pass current at all. Crimp tools come in all configurations and price ranges. A tool in the $.99 bin at the local hardware store is usually worth just that. A good tool will be heavy and won't flex when used. Some tools are designed for special terminals and some even allow you to cut machine screw threads. A good tool will have a die that puts an indention in one side of the connector so the wire will not pull out when crimped.

Soldering can make a better current-flow connection if done correctly, but if not can cause the wire to become brittle and break. Cold joints, which means the joint looks good but the solder didn't flow in the wire strands, are also common. If you do decide to solder the joint, the splice needs tape or heat shrink to finish the job.

Terminals, terminals and more terminals. These high quality crimp terminals are being packaged for wire harness kits ready to be shipped.

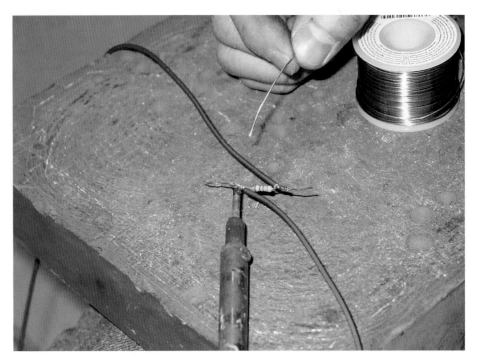

Soldering is a difficult task at times. The wire must be heated and the solder then touched to the wire, instead of the soldering iron tip, for proper flow.

Install Sequence

Project #1:
Wire a 1937 Plymouth

The following sequence of photos shows a typical installation of a chassis harness in a street rod. The car belongs to Jerry Wallace of Arlington, Texas. It is a 1937 Plymouth sedan which he found in Nebraska and rebuilt from the frame up.

Jerry, normally "a hands on" type of guy, decided that a little help with the installation

Roberts checks out the harness Jerry has chosen. A Painless 12 circuit, 10102 kit has all the needed circuits for the car. Jerry decided to keep the car's interior stock in appearance so extra circuits for power windows and locks were not needed. As with all Painless kits, a comprehensive instruction manual is included.

would save him some time even though he knew he could wire the car himself. A phone call to John Roberts and John Nykaza, two street rod friends, was all he needed and they were on the way. A weekend later the car is wired and ready for the glass shop. What does it take to completely rewire a car? Follow along to see exactly what's required.

Tools normally needed include a good standard crimp tool, a double-role crimper for the special Packard-style ter-

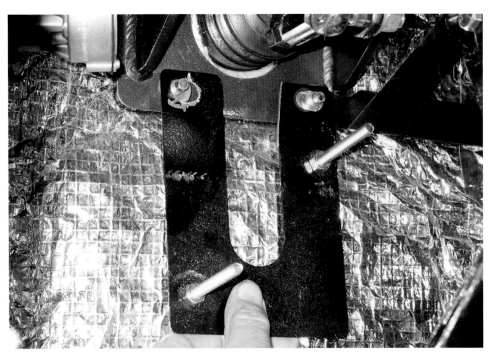

To make the fuse block easily accessible, the decision was made to mount it above the steering column. The brake booster mount bolts made a perfect location for the fuse block bracket which is included in the kit.

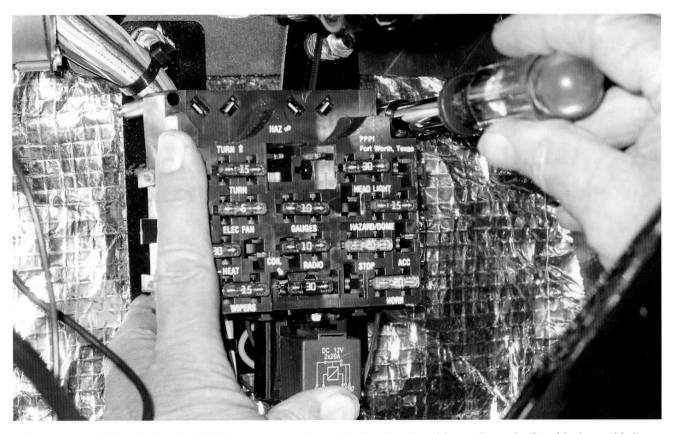

The mounting bolts for the fuse block were inserted into the bracket first, like studs, so the fuse block would slip over them. Nuts were installed and tightened.

The next decision - where to route the wires from the firewall forward? A hole was cut, for the furnished grommet, in the upper left floor pan. That way wire exit behind a body brace out of sight.

The wires in the kit are all marked with their destination as well as being color coded.

In preparation for routing the wires through the floor pan and grommet, Roberts tapes the loose ends with masking tape so they won't get caught or chafe.

Roberts carefully routes the light wiring around the radiator to prevent any chafing or the possibility of the wires getting into the fan.

Once the wires are routed forward through the protective grommet, the light wires have to be separated from the engine wires. The wires are extra long for those custom routing applications.

A piece of rubber hose was installed in the opening between the headlight bucket and the grill housing to help protect the headlight wires.

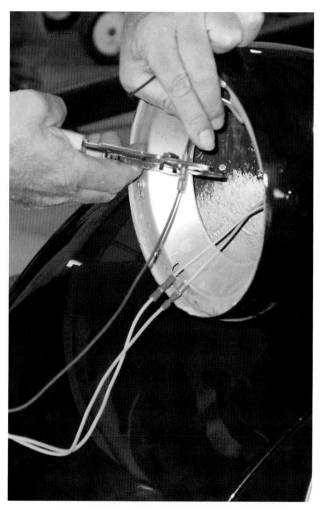

Here you can see the new furnished light pigtails being attached to the harness.

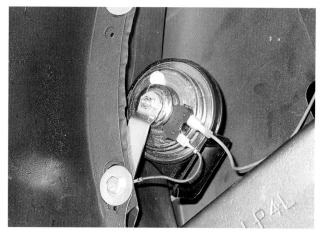

The horn was mounted under the left front fender and wired

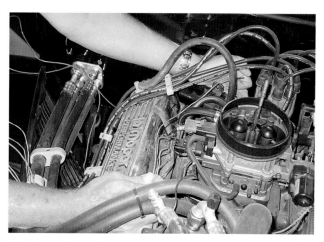

With the front lighting wires completed, the wires for the engine are routed. Insuring the wires are away from moving linkage as well as hot manifolds is important.

The engine temperature, as well as the air conditioning compressor, wires were routed and attached.

minals, nut drivers and small wrenches. A hole saw may be needed to cut the holes in the body so wires can pass through. A small battery charger, one that puts out 10 amps or less, is handy for testing.

As was the case with our Fuel Injection chapter, there are a few additional details concerning the installation that need to be pointed out.

INSTALLATION DETAILS

1. The head light wires were pulled through and then cut to length. The new furnished light pigtails were attached next. Turn signal/park lights were mounted behind the grill and the wires attached.

The distributor wiring was part of the fuel injection harness but the oil pressure sender required a wire.

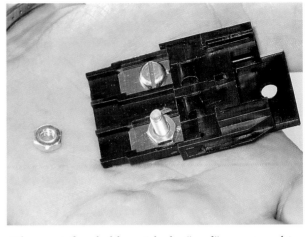

The maxi fuse holder with the "stud" mentioned in the text.

Here you see the wires running to the alternator, including the optional wire included in each Painless kit for high output alternators.

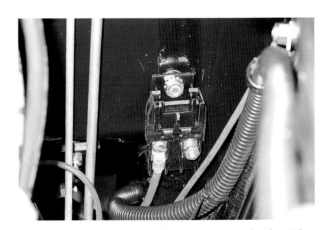

The fuse holder mounted below master cylinder. The fuse block input, A/C power relay input, and extra alternator output wires attach to one side. Other side is attached to the starter solenoid with 8 gauge wire.

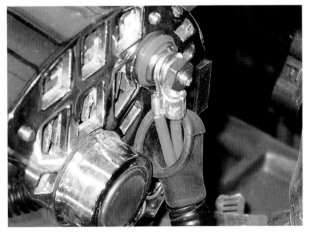

The two output wires are attached to the hot post on the alternator. One goes to the maxifuse, one to the fuse block.

These wires are connected to the neutral safety switch on the Lokar shifter.

With the taillight wires temporarily in position, the dimmer switch wires are cut to length and the special, supplied terminals are crimped on. The terminals will then be installed in a three way plastic housing which will plug onto the switch itself.

2. The maxi fuse holder should be located in a spot easily accessible for wire attachment as well as serviceability. We cut a 10-32 bolt and made it into a stud to allow several wires to be attached to one side of the fuse.

3. Wires are routed down the drivers side valve cover to the alternator. One of the larger red wires is the feed for the fuse block and the other wire is the optional wire included in each Painless kit for high output alternators. This heavy duty output wire runs from the alternator to the maxifuse for maximum charging of high output alternators of 100 amps or more. By adding this wire, the voltage drop in the system is kept to a minimum.

While Roberts was wiring the engine Nykaza was routing the wires for the tail of the car. It's important to tape these wires in place.

The license plate light is in the trunk lid so the brown tail light wire was cut and spliced. The third brake light wire was also routed to the trunk as well as the rear dome light power wire and ground.

The tail lights are slightly modified 37 Ford units and come with wiring pre-attached. Quick disconnect terminals were used between the pigtails and the harness wires on both sides.

The fuel sender wire is tightened in place. When the trunk floor was replaced, a trap door was installed for fuel sender service.

Quick disconnect push-on terminals were installed on the wiper wires and plugged onto the wiper switch.

Jerry wanted map lights so Roberts routes power and ground wires to the windshield header.

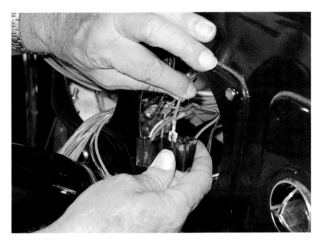

The new Painless headlight switch came with a plastic plug and terminals. Wires were cut to length, terminated, and installed per the instructions.

Due to the fact that several under dash items will need a good ground, Roberts installs a grounding stud in the brake pedal support.

The ignition switch was next. Wires were cut to length and terminated. Accessory wire must go to ACC terminal.

4. The last engine compartment wire is for starter solenoid activation. This wire originated at the ignition switch and is routed to the neutral safety switch (note photos, facing page), cut and attached, then the remaining length of wire was routed to the starter and attached. Different vehicles have this switch located on the transmission, steering column, and sometimes on the shifter like this Lokar unit.

5. As shown, the wires that run to the back of the car are taped to the floor so they can't shift around after the carpet is installed. Care is taken to insure the wires won't be pinched or cut by the seat mounts or trim screws.

6. The last wire in the tail section was the fuel sender wire which was routed through a rubber grommet in the trunk floor and over to the sender.

7. The ignition switch is installed after the headlight switch. Wires were cut to length and terminated with the supplied ring terminals and attached. The accessory wire is attached by itself to the accessory terminal to prevent a back feed to the alternator.

8. The speedometer wires were routed away from the main harness to help prevent any magnetic forces from having an effect on the signal from the sender.

9. The air conditioning system requires an ignition hot wire, included in the Painless harness, to activate the system power relay.

10. The radio is installed behind the glove box door. The harness has a constant and ignition hot wire for radio power.

11. Once the harness is installed, testing of each circuit is done with a small battery charger attached to the battery cables. The small charger is used because of its low amperage output which will not damage any circuitry if there is a problem.

12. LED lights were used in back, and small conventional bulbs up front. Together they create enough current draw to operate the flasher.

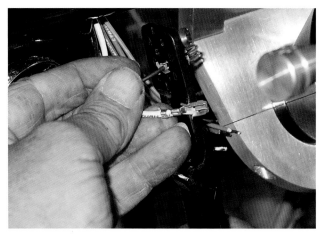

Next are the turn signal switch wires. The IDIDIT column has a GM style plug, so the furnished terminals were crimped on the cut-to-length wires.

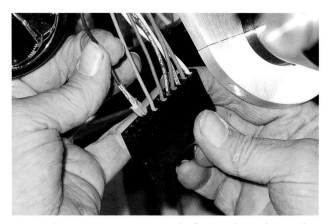

Once the wires are terminated, they're plugged into the mating plastic housing. Housing on column is longer than the furnished plug because column plug was designed for key warning buzzer which is not used.

The gauge wires are attached now as well as the electric speedometer wires.

Roberts attaches the ignition hot wire for the A/C. He also attaches the wire from the thermostat out to the compressor.

The ignition is turned on and the gauges show the appropriate readings.

The radio is hidden behind the glove box door. Quick disconnect terminals are used to aid in easy removal of the radio if necessary.

One last check is the turn signals. LED bulbs were installed in the tail lights and small standard bulbs in the front.

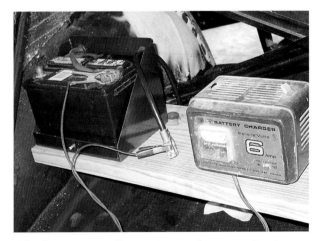

The harness installation is complete so testing is next. For safety reasons, testing is done with a small charger instead of a battery.

Nykaza checks all the circuits, as well as the head lights and everything is a go.

Install Sequence

Project #2, Wire a 1964 Ford

Seen earlier in the book, Lance Overholser's car is a 1964 Ford 2 door sedan Custom 300. Never seen one? Neither had Lance, nor had he ever heard of one. Originally the car had a 289, 2 barrel with a 3 speed tranny but that was soon to change. The 289 ran great so Lance decided to add EFI for drivability (seen in Chapter Seven) and leave the rest of the car's appearance pretty well stock. What couldn't be seen was the wiring. The stock 40 amp generator had to go as well as the wires that couldn't carry the current needed for future creature comfort upgrades. While in the Ft. Worth area, Lance persuaded some of the guys from Painless Performance to aid him in the re-wire of the 64. Probably some refreshments may have been promised, who knows.

Since the car is real basic, a new Painless #20103 muscle car harness was chosen for the job. The install went quickly and the guys from Painless found a few interesting things to add to their tech information books. Follow the photos to see how it all came together.

The new 20103, 12 circuit universal muscle car harness was chosen because it has a bulk head connector for the engine compartment. The car doesn't have a lot of creature comforts (none) so just the basic harness would be enough.

To make the installation easier, the front seat was removed by James Fox, a friend of the tech guys at Painless.

Template in instruction manual is cut out and held to firewall and traced. Hole allows the new bulkhead connector to mate with fuse block inside car.

James now has the challenge of removing the old harness. The under dash wiring wasn't that bad but it wouldn't be long before problems would arise.

With a cutoff tool, a hole was cut to match the template drawing.

The old bulk head plugs were severely corroded. It was a wonder that the car didn't have more electrical problems than it did.

The fuse block is held in place and the mounting bolt holes marked and drilled. The bolts furnished with the kit are installed.

The view of the fuse block mounted to the firewall. Care was taken to insure there's enough clearance for the clutch pedal when depressed

INSTALLATION DETAILS

1. We removed the under dash harness but left the one small harness for the wipers, due to it's good condition. The new wiper power wire will be spliced into this harness.

2. Each wire in the kit is marked with both the circuit and numbers that match the hook up chart in the back of the installation manual.

3. The fuel injection wiring (seen in the Fuel Injection chapter) took care of most of the under-hood wiring, including the coil and distributor. The last item to wire under the hood was the alternator. The old generator was replaced with a new one wire alternator. The exciter wire in the harness, for a 3 wire alternator, was stowed for future use if necessary.

The old headlight wiring as well as the engine wiring was then removed.

James starts routing wires to their final destinations.

With each wire marked with it's circuit and destination, routing becomes very simple.

Brian Montgomery, an engineer at Painless, steps in to help with the routing of the headlight wiring.

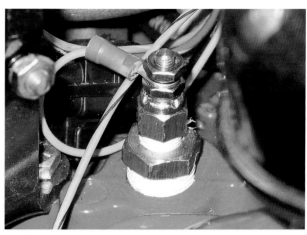

With the lights wired the gauge sending units, like the temperature one shown here, are wired.

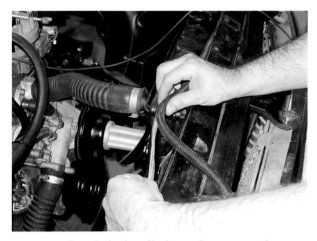

Brian gathered the headlight and turn signal wires into a loom for their protection and routed them across the radiator.

The new oil pressure sending unit was also wired.

The headlight plugs furnished in the kit are spliced onto main harness wires. The original park and turn bulb sockets were spliced in the same manner.

The 2 large wires shown on alternator route to the Maxi fuse and the main harness wire going to the fuse block.

2) Here you see the wires going to the maxi fuse and for the starter relay or solenoid. The fuse holder cover was installed for protection and a clean look.

4. The Maxi fuse holder is wired as follows: The 8 gauge wire, furnished, is routed from one side of the fuse holder to the battery input on the starter relay (solenoid). The other side will get the high output wire from the alternator, the fuse block input wire, and the power input for the EFI computer.

5. To get the Autometer speedo and tach into the pod a little metal had to be removed from the 2 outside holes (note photo, page 124).

6. The gauges came with optional red color covers for the dash lights, they were installed to give the gauges that red hue at night.

7. A bracket was fabricated to hold the new brake light switch, mounted to the brake pedal support. Later, if cruise is added, the dual switch needed for the cruise will fit the same bracket (note photo, page 125).

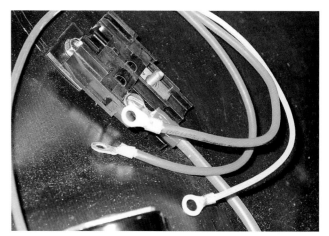

1) The Maxi fuse holder was mounted to the inner fender near the starter relay.

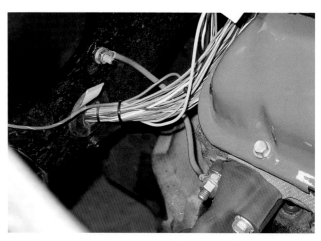

3) A ground wire was routed between the engine and body. This wire is extremely important to prevent gauge fluctuations, and feed back in the dash

4) While the engine wiring was being completed, Lance routed the tail wiring under the carpet and into the trunk area. The wires were held in place by the old stand by, duct tape.

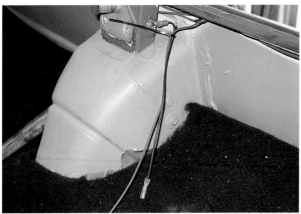

A pigtail was made for the license plate light. The fuel tank sender wire was routed through the floor pan using a small rubber grommet.

With the tach and speedo installed, the rest of the gauges go in using a special plate from Boese Engineering. This plate has provisions for the turn signal and high beam indicators.

Each taillight was wired with bullet style terminals just like the original wiring. These terminals aid in servicing the bulb sockets if ever needed .

With gauges installed, it's time to make a harness, from cut-offs left over from other areas of the car. A Painless quick connect kit, 40011, was installed to allow quick dash removal for servicing.

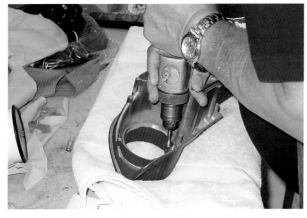

With the rest of the car wired, it's time to focus on the dash. Lance decided to give the dash cluster a sportier look by installing Autometer gauges.

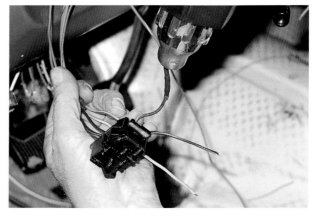

The light switch is wired before the dash is installed, using original switch and connector. Once the wires in the connector are identified, using a continuity tester, the wires are spliced into the harness and covered with heat shrink.

The turn signal switch wires were traced out and connected to the main harness with bullet terminals.

All the switches are wired, so now it's time to install the dash pod. The quick connects are plugged together and the pod is inserted into the dash.

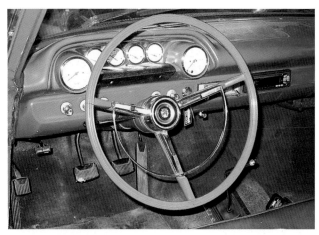

The new dash has a sporty appearance as well as increased visibility.

The brake light switch was moved to the inside of the car due to the new style master cylinder we installed.

Lance turns on the lights as well as other circuits and finds everything is operating fine. Another successful wiring installation, it was Painless.

Chapter Nine

Tips & Troubleshooting

From Dead Batteries to A/C Circuits

No matter how careful you are in buying components and installing the harness, electrical gremlins still crop up. Call it Murphy's law. There is good news, however. Most problems are not as tough to fix as you might think. Before you tear your hair out or begin replacing components willy-nilly, stop and read the information that follows. No matter how mysterious it might seem, there is a logical reason for any electrical problem.

Typical electrical troubles include things like premature battery drain, lights that get brighter

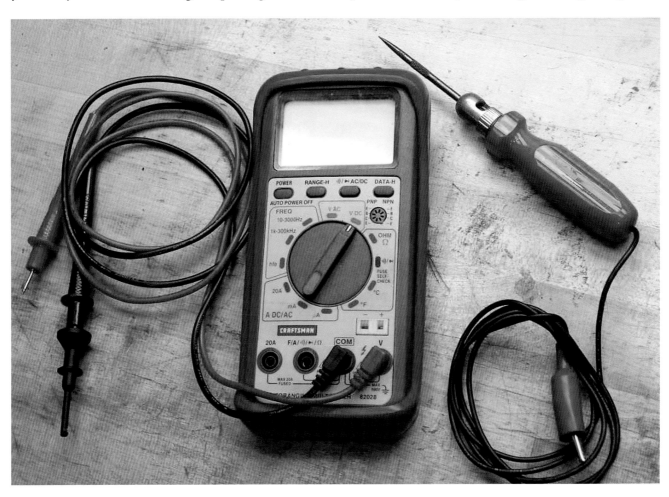

Testing tools, such as a volt-ohm meter and an old fashioned test light, are a must on the work bench when diagnosing problems with an electrical system.

as the engine rpm increases, gauges with erratic readings or a vast array of other gremlins. As with any other task in wiring, trouble shooting requires patience, patience, patience.

TROUBLE SHOOTING, BATTERY DRAIN

Battery drain occurs often when a vehicle sits for extended periods of time. Memory radios, clocks and computers draw a small amount of current at all times. The current draw is usually in milliamps so it takes weeks to drain a fully charged battery in normal circumstances.

Quick draining of a battery can be caused by several different things. The alternator is usually the culprit. A faulty brake switch or dome light switch can also create a problem.

Doing a test to find the problem is quite easy. Disconnect a battery cable and get a standard test light with a sharp probe on one end and a spring loaded clamp on the other. With the battery disconnected, it doesn't matter which cable is removed, probe the battery cable and attach the test light lead clamp on the disconnected cable. If there is a voltage draw, the light will illuminate. Once attached, the light will probably be on. Remove

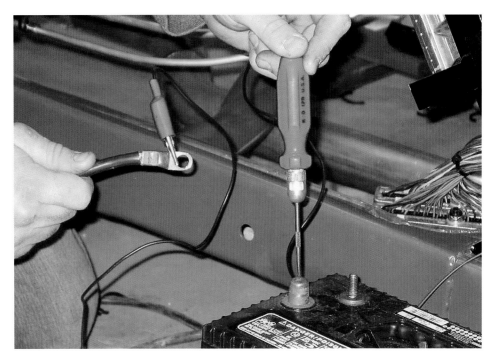

By removing a battery cable and attaching a simple test light in series, you can tell if there is a drain on the electrical system. If light is lit that means there is a circuit that is using current.

Removing the radio fuse will eliminate the radio memory circuit from drawing current. This circuit requires a very small amount of current normally, but some radios require enough to run down a battery in a couple of weeks.

127

By disconnecting the wires at the alternator the alternator can be eliminated as a potential problem. The removal of the plug will check the internal regulator and the removing of the output wire(s) will check the internal diodes.

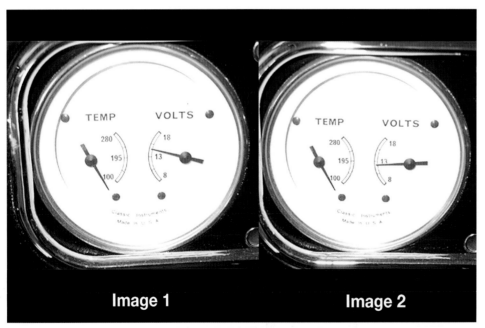

Image 1   Image 2

Image 1 shows a voltmeter reading of about 14 volts. This is normal for most charging systems (13.6 to 14.8) with no excessive load on the electrical system. A slight change of maybe 1 volt will probably occur if the lights are turned on or the windows are rolled up. Image 2 shows a much larger voltage drop. This can be caused by an electrical system that's not capable carrying enough current for a specific load, such as an electric fan.

the fuses from the fuse block that are in the radio and computer circuits. This will stop any draw the memory section of the radio or computer might have.

Is the light still on? If not, the problem is the radio or computer. Light is still on?

Since the alternator is usually the problem, disconnect the wires attached to the alternator and see if the light goes out. Light still on? If it is, leave the alternator disconnected and start removing the remaining fuses in the fuse block one at a time and check the light after each one has been removed. When the one is removed that makes the light go out, that circuit is the one with the problem.

Once the problem has been identified and repaired, re-install the fuses one at a time and check the light to insure it stays out. If the light comes back on you may have more than one problem. Continue this practice until all circuits are re-powered, including the alternator, and then re-fuse the radio and computer.

Once the problem has been found and repaired, reconnect the battery cable.

VOLTAGE DROP PREVENTION

After attending the recent NSRA Street Rod Nationals I came home with several concerns about the electrical systems in Rods that are being built today, but more so of Rods that have been built over the last few years.

Electrical systems and add-on accessories are changing so rapidly and demanding so much more electricity, it is almost impossible to keep up. Alternators are twice the size of ten years ago in an effort to try to keep up with current demand for creature comforts.

I spoke with a rodder who purchased a wiring harness 9 years ago and is just now ready to install it. 9 years ago we had the wonderful 65 amp Delcotron alternator and maybe a small electric fan. The wiring in that harnessing reflects the typical loads of the time. What happens now when we add a 140 amp alternator to power an amp-guzzling electric fan, air conditioning, halogen lights and power for this and that. Then we had an amp gauge that might read 40 amps, today it would go up in smoke in the first 10 minutes - if it lasted that long. Another rodder

If such a drop occurs on your voltmeter a couple of things can be done to locate the draw. First, with the engine running, check the output at the back of the alternator and see if it is the same as what the voltmeter is reading. If it is higher, the problem is excessive load on the fuse center, wiring or ignition switch (most ignition switches have max. capacity of 60 amps). If the output is the same, the belt driving the alternator may be slipping or the alternator may have an internal problem.

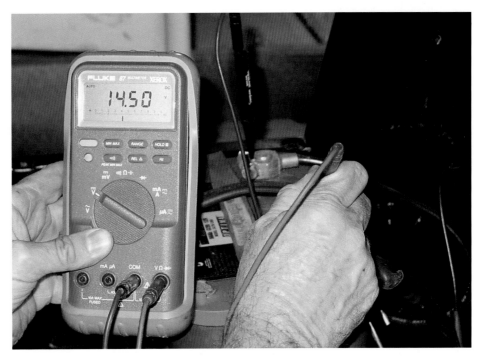

Second, check the voltage at the battery; it should be the same as the alternator output. Here it is shown that the voltage drop is about 2 tenths of a volt which is just fine.

Here a relay mounted on the radiator support for the electric fan. Relays should always be mounted in a direct line between the power source and the load they are controlling. Never pull main current for the relay from the fuse block, always go to a main battery power source such as a Maxi fuse or starter solenoid.

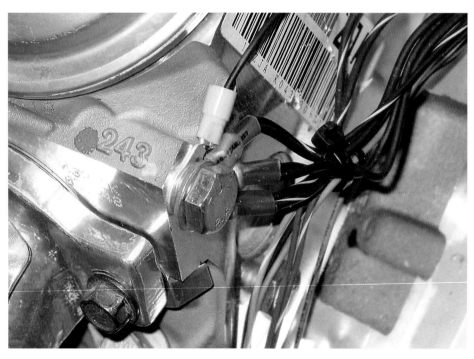

Many grounds, such as in electronic fuel injection, require attachment directly to the engine. These grounds help eliminate electrical noise and spikes.

was having problems with his system. Every time his electric fan came on the voltmeter went to 10 volts and the engine died. His electronic fuel injection computer required 10.5 volts to operate and was starved for current due to the fan.

Voltmeters are today's way of seeing what the vehicle's electrical demands are and how those demands are being met. They can tell us many things, from how the charging system is functioning to whether or not the loads on the wiring are too great. Knowing how to read the voltmeter is the key.

Relays are today's answer to power transfer of current to those hungry creature comforts. Relays are a lot like voltmeters. Proper use will provide relief of worry about what's happening in your electrical system.

With the new 100 amp plus alternators, an additional wire, 10 gauge or larger, between the alternator and the battery source (starter solenoid) is recommended.

If turning off a specific item allows the voltmeter to return to its normal reading, then that item is in need of a relay so current can be supplied directly from the battery source.

What does a relay do? As mentioned earlier, it is a device that transfers electrical current directly from the battery/alternator source to the device (electric fan, air conditioner etc.) instead of through a switch. The switch controlling the device now turns the relay on or off (note the comments in Chapter Five).

Since a relay only requires as much current as a dash light to activate, the load on the switch and its wiring is almost eliminated. The contacts inside the relay are designed to carry high amounts of current and are connected by heavy wires between the power source and the load.

If relays are so good, why aren't they used in more circuits? They should be! In new cars and trucks, relays control almost every circuit.

Proper installation of relays is just as important. Relays require protection from overloads, as any circuit does, which is commonly done with automatic re-set circuit breakers or maxi-fuses. Relays need to be placed as close to a direct line from the power source to the load as possible to prevent any voltage drop. A side benefit is that motors and solenoids will last longer and be more efficient when they are supplied with ample voltage.

An example of the roll proper voltage plays in efficiency is an electric fan. Automobiles operate on direct current (DC). A DC motors' revolutions per minute (rpm) are directionally proportional to voltage. Let's say that your fan has a maximum efficiency rating of 2800 rpm at 14 volts. What happens at 12 volts? 10 volts? The fan probably runs at 2400 and 2000 rpms respectively. Now you know why that green stuff keeps coming from under the radiator cap!

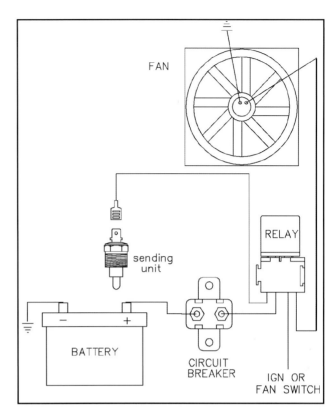

This drawing illustrates the proper wiring of an electric fan relay. Main power should always be provided by a battery source.

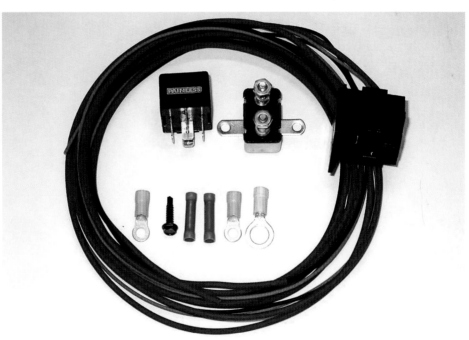

A manual fan relay can be installed to operate the fan by the ignition or a switch in the dash. Power for the fan and relay comes from the battery source, not the fuse block.

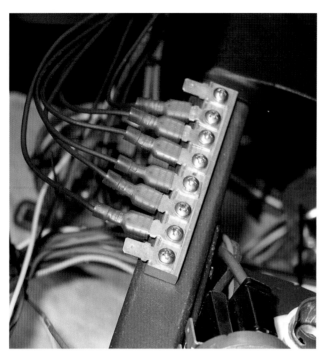

Good grounds are a must on any vehicle. When possible they should connected as shown here, to a body panel or bracket connected to the engine or transmission. Attaching ground lugs directly to the battery will help prevent voltage spikes.

In summary, the electrical system you have purchased today may be out dated in a couple of years. Electronics in automobiles, as in your PC or cell phone, change constantly. Harness manufacturers are constantly up grading wire size, terminals, routing and connections to try to stay ahead of the demands.

If you have a harness more than a couple of years old and are just now installing it in your ride, be safe, contact the manufacturer and be sure it has the upgrades needed to comply with your needs.

GAUGE FLUCTUATION

Gauges are extremely sensitive devices. They can be very accurate or they can give you a reading some where off the map.

Gauges can only give you a reading as accurate as the information they gather from the sending units. The biggest problem encountered is fluctuation when the lights, or another circuit such as the turn signals, are activated. If this is the case, a bad or insufficient ground is the cause. Multiple grounds work the best for individual gauges because of voltage differences each gauge may have. Some times a back feed from the illumination bulbs causes a problem. If the engine does not have a good ground strap to the body and frame the readings from the senders may not be correct.

As mentioned in an earlier chapter, the wires from the sender to the gauge may pick up stray signals (noise) from other circuits and cause an incorrect reading. Electric speedometers are the worst for picking up stray signals.

EFI systems usually have their own fuse block. Due to the complexity of the systems, they require several fuses and relays. The only requirement of the main chassis harness, for these systems, is an ignition power source.

ELECTRONIC FUEL INJECTION

With electronic fuel injection there can be a multitude of problems, from not starting to terrible drivability. Since there are so many different systems, only a couple of symptoms will be addressed.

An engine that will not start is the most common problem. The cause in most cases (electrically) is the power wire from the ignition switch to the computer. The computer requires power in the start and run positions of the switch. Many switches have internal segments that do not provide power to the ignition during cranking. A test light will tell you if the computer ignition power wire is properly connected. The check engine light, if present, should also stay on in the crank and run positions.

The second most common problem is an engine that starts and dies. Most computers since 1989 have (VATS) vehicle anti-theft system. With out a re-programmed chip or computer, the engine's injector pulse signal will be shut off within the first few seconds after starting. If spark is present during cranking but the engine will not start, the injectors are not pulsing.

As a side note, if the engine has been sitting for a long period of time, 6 months or more, the injectors can be gummed up and won't pulse. The fuels of today turn to varnish very quickly. A slight tap with a medium size hammer handle may jar them enough to free up the plunger.

For more information on how to troubleshoot your vehicles EFI system contact Painless Performance's Tech services.

AIR CONDITIONING CIRCUITS

For some insight into the unique wiring requirements needed for an air conditioning installation we contacted Jack Chisenhall, President of Vintage Air in San Antonio, Texas. Vintage Air designs and manufactures air conditioning kits for everything from '87 Chevy pickup trucks to '32 Fords. Jack began the discussion by pointing out the major differences between the various types of cars.

"You need to make a distinction between the way you would approach the air conditioning wiring for a later model car like a '55 Chevy or a Muscle car, and a scratch built hot rod type vehicle.

"Most OEM harnesses for those cars from the 50's and 60's simply don't have enough capacity to draw the power for the air conditioning through the fuse block. All of our standard wiring harnesses include two breakers and two relays, this way we aren't drawing the current from the factory fuse block. We only use one existing low-current circuit to turn on, or excite the relay when the ignition is turned on. With a scratch built car that doesn't use an OEM style harness, how you power the air conditioning depends on the situation and how much capacity the wiring harness has. Some of the wiring harnesses are designed to accommodate air conditioning."

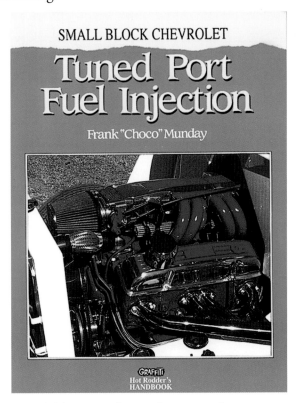

Available at Painless Performance, this is an idiot-proof guide to installing the entire GM TPI system, into Hot Rods, Street Machines, Kemps, 4WD, Jags and other conversions.

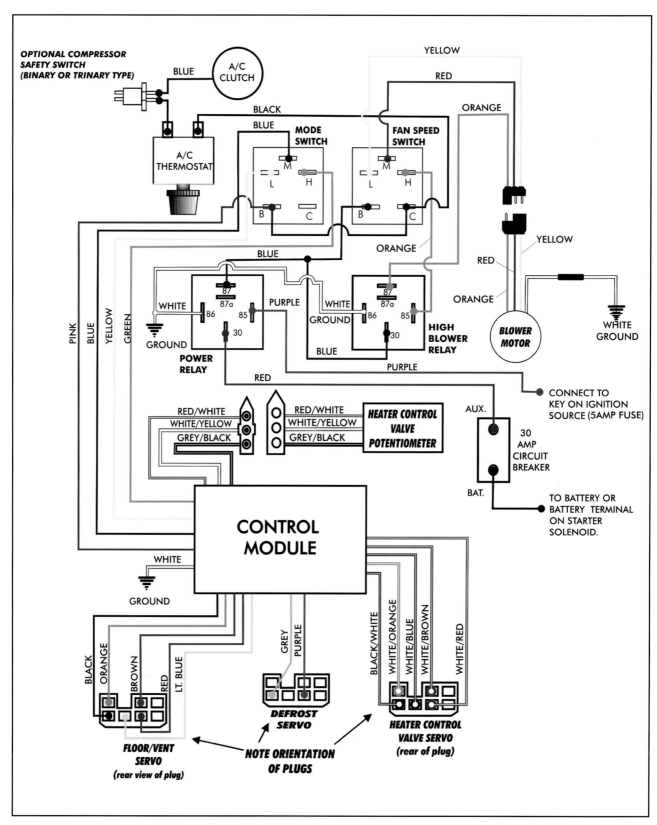

*This current Gen II wiring diagram uses 4 relays and a binary, or tertiary, switch to protect the compressor.
Vintage Air*

Discussion of air conditioning wiring always brings up the subject of cooling fans. More and more hot Rodders are turning to electric cooling fans in place of the engine driven fan. "Some of those electric fans just aren't good enough," explains Jack. "They may cool a motor just fine, but they won't provide enough air flow to properly remove heat from the radiator and the air conditioning condenser."

The other mistake people make is to install an electric fan in an air conditioned car and control the fan solely with the engine temperature sensor. To quote Jack again, "By the time that engine is hot enough to turn on the cooling fan, the air conditioning is probably having a problem - the high side pressure is probably already way too high."

More and more of the air conditioning kits that ship from the Vintage Air plant include a three-way (trinary) switch located in the system's high pressure side. This switch protects the system against very high or low pressure and also turns on the electric fan when pressure on the high side of the system hits a pre-determined figure (255 psi).

Exactly how you wire the air conditioning will

Hood sides with louvers allow the hot air to escape the engine compartment. Smoothie hood sides are attractive, but they may not allow enough air movement to cool the engine.

This large cooling fan and shroud covers almost all of the radiator. Maximum cooling requires air flow across as much of the radiator as possible. The shroud enhances the draw of air. Pullers work better than pushers.

depend on the system you install. Aftermarket kits like those from Vintage Air come with their own wiring diagrams. We do provide a few sample air conditioning wiring schematics, provided by Vintage Air, so you can see how the three-way switch, the cooling fan, and the air conditioning circuits are typically wired.

ELECTRIC COOLING FANS AND AIRFLOW

Part of this material is taken from the Jack Chisenhall/Tim Remus book: How To Air Condition Your Car.

Before jumping into the subject of cooling fans we need to consider the larger issue of airflow (even if it does seem slightly outside the realm of wiring). An efficient cooling system is only as good a its ability to give up heat to the air moving through the radiator. Some cars (hot rods in particular) have trouble moving enough air over the radiator. The typical V-8 radiator and air conditioning condenser needs a mini-

mum of 2300 CFM of air moving over it for adequate cooling.

Good airflow is more than just a matter of presenting the full face of the radiator to the air in front of the radiator or grille. The air won't move through the radiator unless the pressure on the back side is lower than the pressure on the front of the radiator. Street rods with smooth sided hoods often provide no good way for the air to exit the engine compartment, no matter what you do with the fan or fans. The final result is a lack of airflow over the radiator and a car that runs hot.

The hood and hood sides need to be part of the overall plan for the vehicle. If the air can't exit the sides of the hood, it must exit below the engine compartment. Sometimes a simple air-dam near the front axle can effectively create a low pressure area behind the radiator and solve an overheating problem by moving more air

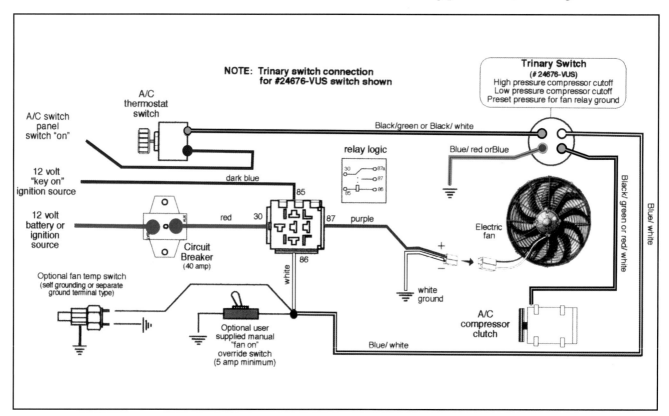

With the use of a trinary switch, wired as shown, there are 3 ways to turn on the cooling fan: manually, with the thermostatic switch mounted in the radiator, or with the tertiary switch itself. The trinary switch also cuts power to the A/C clutch when the high-side pressure is too high or too low. Vintage Air

through the engine compartment.

The fan you use is obviously part of the airflow discussion. Before installing an electric fan(s), consider the following fact: A belt-driven fan, operating with a properly designed shroud, will generally move more air than one or two electric fans – all other factors being equal.

A shroud improves the efficiency of a fan (any fan) enormously. Think of it as a funnel, making it possible for the fan to pull more air, more evenly, over the entire surface of the radiator. Even a simple "ring" shroud will improve air movement across the radiator and provide a significant improvement in airflow.

Electric fans have the advantage of only coming on when they are specifically needed and drawing no power and no horsepower when they aren't. Though they may not move as much total air as a good belt-driven fan, electric fans will often fit in places much too tight for good conventional fan.

The first rule of electric fans is: try to pull the air, not push it. Pusher fans, mounted in front of the radiator and condenser, obstruct the airflow all the time, whether they're working or not. The second rule

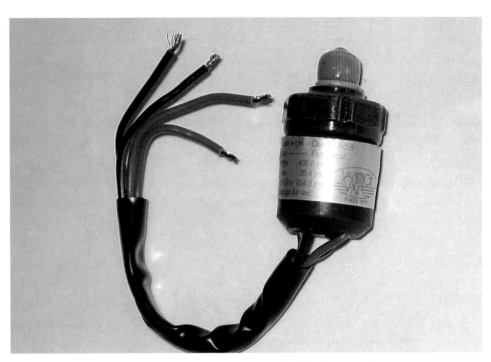

The trinary switch, like this one from Vintage Air, uses the low and high pressure of the air conditioning system to control the compressor clutch as well as the electric fan.

Designed to ground the relay controlling the cooling fan, these thermostatic switches come with an adapter and are available in either 190 or 210 degree calibrations. Vintage Air

is: always run the fan(s) off a thermostat, not off a manual switch, because it's too easy to forget to turn the fan on in a traffic situation and cook the motor.

As was mentioned earlier in the book, the simplest electric fan set ups (in a car without air conditioning) use a thermostat mounted in the radiator lower tank or the engine, to sense the coolant temperature. When the coolant reaches a certain temperature – meaning it wasn't cooled sufficiently during its pass through the radiator – the sensor turns on the fan. The fan draws air over the radiator and removes heat from the water passing through the radiator. The sensor is typically used to control a relay. Usually the sen-

sor provides the ground for the control side of the relay. Power for the control side can come from an ignition-on or constant-hot power source. The advantage of using a constant-hot power source for the control side is the fact that the cooling fan will run after you shut off the car, to help dissipate the heat-soak that often occurs after the car or truck is shut off on a hot summer day.

When an electric fan(s) is used on a car with air conditioning, it must be integrated with the air conditioning as well as the cooling system. On a hot day with a cool engine idling and the air conditioning on, the pressure in the high side of the air conditioner can rise very rapidly. The high side pressure can go as high as 400 or 500 psi, enough to rupture a hose or blow the hose off the fitting. You need a high side switch that turns on the fan(s) at about 250 psi, thus moving fresh air over the condenser and lowering the pressure (temperature and pressure are closely related, as the temperature comes down so does the pressure).

When installing an electric fan, use a temperature sensor that goes into the lower (or cooler) radiator tank (or the engine) and avoid sensors that clamp to the outside of the radiator. An adjustable temperature sensor is a nice feature.

The high side switch can be a multi-function switch like that mentioned earlier. The three-way switch from Vintage Air has three functions: 1. To act as a high side fan switch. 2. To function as a high side cutout, cutting power to the compressor clutch if for any reason the pressure goes above 405 psi. 3. To act as a low-pressure cutout, cutting power to the compressor clutch when the pressure gets very low, less than 30 psi), meaning a loss of refrigerant and lubricant as well.

This compact and versatile electric fan for the limited budget is designed for lower cooling requirements in primary and auxiliary applications. Flex-A-Lite

Rick Love from Vintage Air reports that there's another mistake they often see on street rods and hot rods. "The electric fan is wired to come on whenever the compressor is engaged. This is definitely the wrong way to wire the fan. With an engine temperature switch and a tri-nary switch properly connected, the engine and Air conditioning system will engage the fan when more airflow is needed. There is no reason to run an electrical fan while cruising down the highway, it runs the fan needlessly, and can even disrupt airflow."

The fan you buy should be the biggest one that will fit your particular application. The blades near the hub of a fan don't move much air – nearly all the work the fan does is done near the tips of the blades. As the blade gets longer, the percentage of blade that is away from the hub increases and the speed of the blade tip increases – making for a fan that can move significantly more air. Some of the newest designs incorporate their own ring-style shroud, a nice feature that will improve the fan's ability to move air.

Jack Chisenhall warns potential fan buyers to use caution when buying fans, as not all cooling fans are created equal. To quote Jack, "Many of the fans simply aren't good enough, they're meant to cool the engine or act as secondary fans. You have to be sure the unit you buy is designed to provide adequate airflow for the engine *and* the air conditioning condenser. You have to know what the capacity of the fan is. Sometimes the only way to be sure you're getting a good enough fan is to buy from a good reputable supplier.

"The best fans have large diameter, broad blades and they have a relatively high wattage rating. Because the amperage draw is significant, a good fan needs a proper circuit. Some of the big ones draw 25 to 30 amps, and 35 amps at start up."

As we've said before, wiring your fan is just like wiring any other accessory. Use a thermostatic switch to turn it on and off, and pull the power through a relay.

ENGINE STARTER SLUGGISH OR NOT OPERATING

Starters, especially ones with the solenoid mounted on them, often fail to operate when hot. This can be caused by several different things. The most common is old wiring that can't provide the amount of current required by the solenoid. Another problem occurs when the solenoid gets hot and expands, and the internal plunger locks or sticks in its bore. If this hap-

Curved blade fans are becoming more popular. They move lots of air and are relatively quiet. Flex-A-Lite

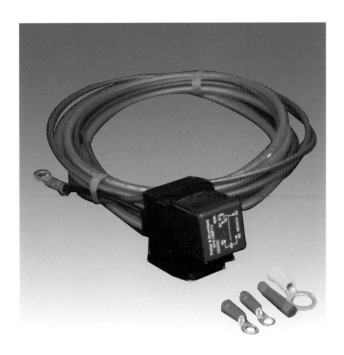

Hot shot relay kits are available to apply battery power directly to the solenoid activation terminal. This allows the solenoid to function even when it is hot. Painless

Special LED flashers are now available that will allow the use of LED lights front and rear. They have a load circuit built in eliminating the need for an exterior load, or bulb, in the circuit. The ground wire routes the extra load to ground. Painless

pens, even more current is required by the windings to pull the plunger. The other possibility is that the starter is worn out.

A simple test to check the starter is to jump the battery post and the solenoid activation post with a screwdriver. If the starter works properly, it's not the starter. Warning, before doing this test insure that the transmission is in neutral and the ignition is off.

If the starter seems to be functioning properly, a hot starter relay may solve the problem. This relay kit, made by Painless, mounts in the starter area and provides power from the battery cable directly to the solenoid activation post.

FLASHERS WILL NOT FLASH

You have installed new LED tail lights and now they will not flash. The LED lights do not draw enough current to make the bimetallic strip in the flasher heat up and bend. In most cases a 1034 or 1157 bulb in the front will have enough current draw to allow the flasher to operate. If not, or you have LED lights front and back, a load will need to be placed in the circuit to create enough current draw to trip the flasher. A high current resistor or a 1187 bulb put in series with the flasher circuit are common solutions. LED flashers are now on the market which has the load inside the case. These units simply plug in as an ordinary flasher and usually provide enough load.

TURN SIGNAL INDICATOR LIGHT MALFUNCTION

A turn signal light staying on or glowing dimly, can tell us a lot about the lighting system. If you have a signal light that comes on

when the park, or head-
lights, are on that means a
grounding problem in that
side of the vehicle. It could
be front or rear but usually
a quick visual check to see
which light isn't on will tell
you where the problem is.
Do both lights come on
when you hit the brake?
This is caused by the indicator lights being attached
to the rear light (brake)
wires instead of the front
turn wires.

BRAKE LIGHT SWITCH FAILURE

Brake light switches
have a couple of common causes for failure.
Brake switches are designed to carry no more
than about 10 amps of current. If you have
halogen tail/brake lights, they will pull as much
as 25 amps and burn out
the switch prematurely.

Hydraulic switches are
easy to install in a brake
line but they have a flaw.
With all the pressure in
today's disc brake systems,
the extra pressure will leak
around the internal
diaphragm and fill the air
cavity (which is what allows
the diaphragm to move).
With brake fluid on both
sides of the diaphram,
you've created a hydraulic
lock. Regardless of the
pedal pressure the dia-
phragm can't move and the
internal electrical contacts
can't make contact. This is
the reason hydraulic switches haven't been in production cars for years

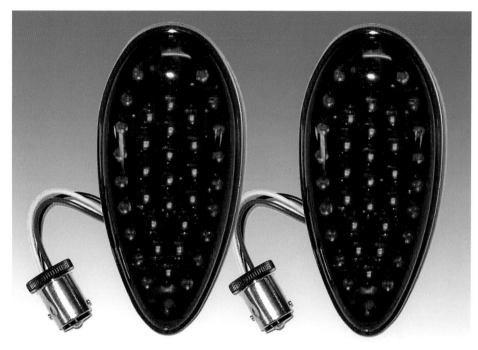

*LED lights, like this 39 Ford tail light, are becom-
ing more popular. They have increased light output,
less current draw as well as a cooler operation temperature. Painless*

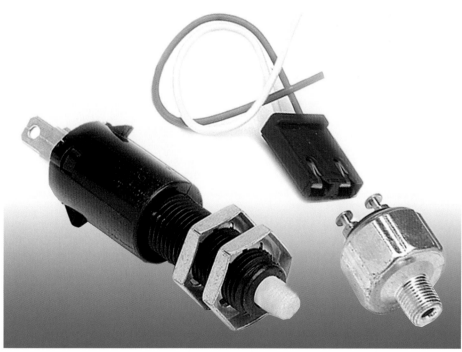

*Hydraulic brake switches are common on today's hot rods. Problems do occur,
due to the increased line pressure of today's disc brake systems. Which is why
many rodders run a simple mechanical switch. Painless*

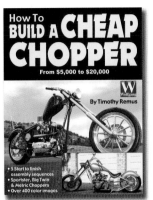

HOW TO BUILD A CHEAP CHOPPER

Choppers don't have to cost $30,000. In fact, a chopper built from the right parts can be assembled for as little as $5,000. *How to Build a Cheap Chopper* documents the construction of 4 inexpensive choppers with complete start-to-finish sequences photographed in the shops o Donnie Smith, Brian Klock and Dave Perewitz.

Least expensive is the metric chopper, based on a Japanese 4-cylinder engine and transmission installed in an hardtail frame. Next up, price wise, are 2 bikes built using Buell/Sportster drivetrains. The recipe here is simple, combine one used Buell or Sportster with a hardtail frame for an almost instant chopper. The big twin chopper is the least cheap of the 4, yet it's still far less expensive than most bikes built today.

Twelve Chapters   144 Pages $24.95   Over 400 photos-100% color

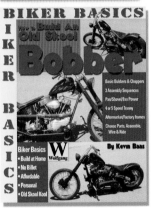

HOW TO BUILD AN OLD SKOOL BOBBER

New from Wolfgang Publications comes Biker Basics, a series of how-to books designed to help men and women with average mechanical skills and only a modest budget build and customize motorcycles.

You don't need thirty thousand dollars or a Bridgeport mill - just enough money to buy some used parts, enough drive to finish the project, and a copy of this new book from Wolfgang Publications
• This book is a throwback to the days when a custom motorcycle was a machine nearly any motorhead could assemble in the garage from swap-meet parts using hand tools and common sense.
• Your guide to Old Skool Kool.
• Just say no to theme bikes.
• Build it cheap, build it right.

Ten Chapters   144 Pages $24.95   Over 500 photos - 100% color

ADVANCED AIRBRUSH ART HOW TO SECRETS FROM THE MASTERS

Like a video done with still photography, this new book from Wolfgang Publications is made up entirely of photo sequences that illustrate each small step in the creation of an airbrushed masterpiece. Watch as well-known masters like Vince Goodeve, Chris Cruz, Steve Wizard and Nick Pastura start with a sketch and end with a NASCAR helmet or motorcycle tank covered with graphics, murals, pin-ups or all of the above.

Interviews explain each artist's preference for paint and equipment, and secrets learned over decades of painting. Projects include a chrome eagle surrounded by reality flames, a series of murals, and a variety of graphic designs.

This is a great book for anyone who takes airbrushing seriously and wants to learn more.

Ten Chapters   144 Pages $24.95   500 color images - 100% color

PROFESSIONAL AIRBRUSH TECHNIQUES

Written by well-known Airbrush artist Vince Goodeve, this new book uses 144 pages and over 500 color images to explain a lifetime's worth of learning. Follow Vince through multiple photo sequences that explain his choice of color, sense of design and preference for tools and materials. Early chapters explain shop set up and preparations of the metal canvas. Ten start-to-finish sequences walk the reader through Vince's airbrush work with both motorcycles and cars. Projects include simple graphics as well as complex and intricate designs. Accustomed to teaching, Vince uses a style that is easy to follow and understand. His enthusiasm for the airbrush comes through, making the text easy to follow. Vince Goodeve has something to say to all airbrush artists – whether beginner or advanced.

Ten Chapters   144 Pages $24.95   Over 400 color photos- 100% color

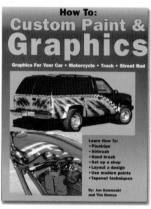

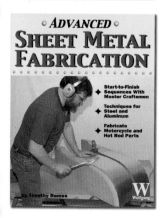

Sources

Autometer
413 West Elm St.
Sycamore, IL 60178
815.899.0800
Fax: 815.895.6786
www.autometer.com

Classic Instruments
1299 M-75 South
Boyne City, MI 49712
231.582.0461
Fax: 231.582.3114
www.classicinstruments.com

Dakota Digital
4510 W. 61st St. N.
Sioux Falls, SD 57107
605.332.6513
www.dakotadigital.com

Fifth Ave. Antique Auto
415 Court St.
Clay Center, KS 64732
785.632.3450
www.fifthaveinternetgarage.com

Flex-A-Lite
7213 45th Ct. E.
Fife, WA 98424
253.922.2700
Fax: 253.248.9112

Painless Performance
2501 Ludelle St.
Ft. Worth, TX 76105
817.244.6212
Fax: 817.244.4024
www.painlessperformance.com

Powermaster
7501 Strawberry Plains Pike
Knoxville, TN 37924
865.688.5953
Fax: 865.281.9844
www.powermastermotorsports.com

Tuff Stuff Performance
9004 Madison Avenue
Cleveland, Ohio 44102
216.961.1800
1.800.331.6562
Fax: 216.961.1868
www.tuffstuffperformance.com

Vintage Air
18865 Goll St.
San Antonio, TX 78266
210.654.7171
Fax: 210.654.3113
www.vintageair.com